Breakthroughs

An Integrated Advanced English Program

Workbook

Marina Engelking   **Gloria McPherson-Ramirez**

OXFORD

UNIVERSITY PRESS

OXFORD
UNIVERSITY PRESS
70 Wynford Drive, Don Mills, Ontario M3C 1J9

www.oupcan.com

Oxford New York
Athens Auckland Bangkok Bogota Buenos Aires
Calcutta Cape Town Chennai Dar es Salaam Delhi
Florence Hong Kong Istanbul Karachi Kuala Lumpur
Madrid Melbourne Mexico City Mumbai Nairobi Paris
São Paulo Singapore Taipei Tokyo Toronto Warsaw

and associated companies in
Berlin Ibadan

Oxford is a trademark of Oxford University Press

Canadian Cataloguing in Publication Data

Engelking, Marina, 1959-
    Breakthroughs: an integrated advanced English
    program. Workbook

ISBN 0-19-541254-0

1. English language - Problems, exercises, etc.
I. McPherson-Ramirez, Gloria, 1963- . II. Title.

PE1112.E54 1997 Suppl. 2   428   C97-932171-9

Cover art: Susan Leopold
Illustrations: Suzanne Mogensen
Editor: Trish Brown
Compositor: Indelible Ink

This book is printed on permanent (acid-free) paper. ∞

Printed and bound in Canada

4   01

Contents

UNIT 1
The Calm Before the Storm

Exercise A

Rewrite each sentence below using one of the following words. Notice how the use of precise vocabulary eliminates the need for extra words and allows you to express the meaning of the sentences and the images they convey in a simpler way.

erupted	twister	blinding
torrential	epicentre	eye
aftershocks	poisonous gases	fissures

EXAMPLE: The rain, which was coming down extremely hard and fast, soaked Harold to the skin.

The torrential rain soaked Harold to the skin.

1. The snow was coming down so hard we couldn't see to drive, so we pulled off the road.

_____

_____

2. At 10:45 p.m. last night, lava shot out of the mouth of the volcano.

_____

_____

3. A swirling circle of air current touched down and destroyed everything in its path.

_____

_____

4. The earthquake caused great cracks in the earth to open.

_____

_____

5. The volcano emitted fumes that were harmful and deadly.

_____

_____

6. The point at the centre of the earthquake was the coast of Los Angeles.

_____

_____

7. The series of tremors after the main quake were strong enough to rattle the dishes.

_____

_____

8. The point at the centre of the hurricane is calm and quiet.

_____

_____

Exercise B

Fill in the blanks in the following sentences with a word from the list below.

exacerbation	unprecedented	propagate
menacing	recurrence	perennial
havoc	drought	scourge
adverse		

1. The severe _____ in the prairie provinces has cost farmers millions in lost crops.

2. Due to the _____ snowfall, the city has already exhausted its budgeted funds, and winter isn't over yet.

3. The clearing of many forests is an _____ to the problem with the water table.

4. _____ plants are more expensive than annuals, but unlike annuals they grow again every spring.

5. The _____ of floods in certain regions is predictable due to known flood plains.

6. The hailstorm wreaked _____ on the farmers' fields, flattening many hectares of corn.

7. Crops require a certain amount of rain in the spring in order to _____ .

8. _____ swarms of locusts have destroyed whole fields of crops.

9. Forests should be replanted to address the _____ effects of clear-cutting.

10. Droughts have caused a great _____ to African societies, destroying precious food supplies and depriving the nations of much-needed water.

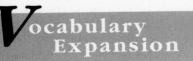

Vocabulary Expansion

Exercise C — Adjective-noun collocations

When describing the weather, certain adjectives are commonly used. Match the adjectives in Column A with the nouns in Column B. Some adjectives may be used with more than one noun. Write a sentence for each adjective-noun collocation on a separate sheet.

Column A	Column B
blinding	breeze
freezing	rain
driving	snow
pouring	wind
spitting	
drizzling	
pelting	
powdery	
strong	
gale-force	
light	
pleasant	
north-easterly	
granular	
packing	
heavy	

Exercise D

The following words describe the intensity of certain types of weather. Write the words in the lines provided above the bar line, positioning them according to their degree of intensity. Words that describe a lesser intensity should be placed at the lighter-coloured end of the bar line and words describing a greater intensity should be positioned at the darker end.

1. RAIN: downpour / mist / drizzle / spitting

_____ _____ _____ _____

2. SNOW: packing / powdery / heavy / light / blinding

_____ _____ _____ _____ _____

3. WIND: gale-force / strong / light / high

_____ _____ _____ _____

Grammar Focus 1

PASSIVE VOICE

Exercise A

Change active voice to passive voice in the following sentences.

1. Scientists who study the earth's atmosphere have issued predictions of impending doom for the past few years.

   _____

   _____

2. A gradual rise in worldwide temperatures has caused global warming.

   _____

   _____

3. Individual researchers made statements that human activity has contributed to global warming.

   _____

   _____

4. The world must take drastic steps to reduce the emissions of heat-trapping gases.

   _____

   _____

5. Rising oceans will flood huge tracts of densely populated land.

   _____

   _____

6. Complex computers simulate the effects of carbon dioxide emissions, methane, and chlorofluoro-carbons.

   _____

   _____

Exercise B

Change passive voice to active voice in the following sentences.

1. The effects of global warming can be masked by the aerosols which cool the planet by blocking the sun.

   _____

   _____

2. Many beaches will be submerged by water from melting glaciers.

_____

_____

3. Temperature and rainfall patterns will be affected by global warming.

_____

_____

4. Our world climate is influenced by deep ocean currents.

_____

_____

5. Emissions must be reduced to the same levels as in the 1920s.

_____

_____

6. The lead role in reducing global warming must be taken by the industrialized nations.

_____

_____

Exercise C

Review the functions of the passive voice on page 5 of your Student Book. What function does the passive voice have in the following sentences?

> (1) Fear-inspiring crocodiles can be found in Kakadu National Park. (2) The shallow water at the border of the park is used as a natural food trap by these prehistoric beasts. (3) Barramundi, giant fish that are native to the area, are reputed to be the best sport fish in the world. (4) The large ones that are too slow crossing the shallow border are attacked and eaten by the giant, log-like crocodiles. (5) Now these great animals are being threatened by miners hoping to extract rich uranium deposits. (6) Ninety thousand tonnes, Australia's biggest deposit of uranium, is located within the borders of Kakadu.

(1) _____

(2) _____

(3) _____

(4) _____

(5) _____

(6) _____

Exercise D

When the passive voice is used, the agent can often be omitted. The agent is included when the agent is unexpected or it is important that it be identified. Circle the agents in the following sentences and cross them out where possible.

1. The need for increased government protection of the environment in Australia has been identified by scientists.

2. Countless articles have been written by David Suzuki condemning our treatment of the environment.

3. Native myths explaining the forces of nature have been recorded by people.

4. The results of the greenhouse effect have been grossly miscalculated by scientists.

5. Impending changes in climate can be predicted by humans through observing animals.

Grammar In Use
Exercise E

Public notices often contain the passive voice. This impersonal structure gives a formal tone to the message. Look at the following notices and determine where each notice might be found.

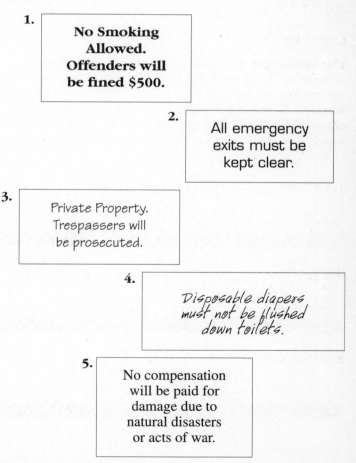

1.
No Smoking Allowed. Offenders will be fined $500.

2.
All emergency exits must be kept clear.

3.
Private Property. Trespassers will be prosecuted.

4.
Disposable diapers must not be flushed down toilets.

5.
No compensation will be paid for damage due to natural disasters or acts of war.

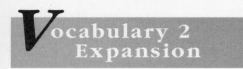

Exercise A

Complete the weather proverbs by matching the first half of the proverb in Column A with the second half in Column B.

Column A	Column B
1. If Groundhog Day be fair and clear...	**a.** ...there'll be a flood.
2. A pale green sky...	**b.** ...March and April will pay full dear.
3. In January should sun appear...	**c.** ...there'll be two winters in the year.
4. When around the moon there's a ring...	**d.** ...the weather it will sting.
5. If a hen crows...	**e.** ...means the wind is high.

In your own words, explain the meaning of each proverb. Add a proverb with which you are familiar that predicts weather conditions.

Exercise B

Nature-related idioms are common. Write definitions / explanations for the idioms underlined in the following sentences.

1. It's <u>raining cats and dogs</u> out there. Unless you have a raincoat and an umbrella, you're going to get soaked.

2. Kim spent all Alain's money and then <u>left him high and dry</u> with a lot of bills to pay and no money.

3. Lucas did an amazing <u>snow job</u> on his mother. She actually believed him when he told her the teacher said he didn't have to attend classes on Fridays.

4. Gaitree likes to sit around and <u>shoot the breeze</u> with her co-workers at lunch in order to keep up on all the latest news.

5. Our dream of owning our own house <u>bit the dust</u> because we just couldn't make it financially feasible.

6. I want to <u>hit the hay</u> early tonight. I haven't been to bed before midnight all week.

7. Habib <u>went out on a limb</u> to start his new business. I hope that the financial risk he is taking pays off handsomely.

8. I'll <u>take a rain check</u> for that invitation. Unfortunately, I already have plans for Saturday. How about Monday?

Grammar Focus 2

PASSIVE VOICE TENSES
Exercise A

Change the following active verbs into passive voice and create a sentence using each verb. Identify the tense of the sentence.

EXAMPLE: purchased: was / were purchased = past tense

The land was purchased by an environmental protection group.

1. recorded

2. control

3. are destroying

4. were ignoring

_____

_____

5. have observed

_____

_____

_____

6. had decided

_____

_____

_____

7. will develop

_____

_____

_____

Exercise B

Rewrite the following sentences by beginning each one with the words provided in parentheses.

1. The First Nations peoples created a myth about five beautiful maidens to explain the origin of Niagara Falls. (A myth)

_____

_____

2. A wild boar gave Anishiniba back his life. (Anishiniba)

_____

_____

3. The Aboriginal people of Australia consider Ayers Rock a spiritual place. (Ayers Rock)

_____

_____

4. The Inuit carved blocks out of snow to build igloos. (Blocks)

_____

_____

5. Powerful spirits control the weather. (The weather)

_____

_____

Exercise C

Choose whether to use the active or passive form of the verbs in parentheses and then write your choice in the blanks provided.

David Suzuki (1) _____ (be) a champion of environmental protection. He supports the notion that environmental education must (2) _____ (teach) from cradle to grave and must (3) _____ (become) part of a required curriculum for engineers, agriculturalists, teachers, lawyers and anyone else who (4) _____ (make) decisions affecting the environment. The knowledge must (5) _____ (be) current so ongoing programs must (6) _____ _____ (develop and study). People must (7) _____ (unlearn) the bad habits of consumption and exploitation practised by our ancestors. Individual responsibility must (8) _____ (take). It's imperative that we understand nature and that it become part of our heart and soul. Long-term rather than short-term strategies must (9) _____ (embrace).

Grammar In Use
Exercise D

The following tips on reducing the amount of garbage you throw out have been written in a very impersonal style using several passive structures. Garbage is a serious threat to our environment. In order to persuade people to reduce their garbage output, rewrite the tips in a less impersonal tone, using the active voice where possible.

Six things to be done to reduce garbage output.

EXAMPLE:

1. Ensure that all papers have been separated for recycling.
   Separate all papers.

2. Bottles, cans, and jars should be put in the recycling box.
   _____

3. Reusable cotton bags should be used for groceries rather than plastic bags.
   _____

4. Food scraps must be placed in a composter.
   _____

5. Disposable diapers quickly fill landfills. Cloth diapers should be used.
   _____

6. Unwanted items in good condition should be donated to charities.
   _____

Grammar Expansion

In informal or spoken English, "get" can substitute for "be" as the auxiliary verb in the passive voice.

EXAMPLE: Jolene **was selected** because of her knowledge of volcanoes.

Jolene **got selected** because of her knowledge of volcanoes.

"Get" is used in the passive voice in informal situations when:

- the process is being emphasized.
  The garbage gets picked up twice a week.

- the subject is animate.
  David Suzuki got fired for his opinions.

- the situation is bad.
  Over one hundred people got killed in that quake.

Exercise E

Complete the following sentences using appropriate forms of the verbs "to be" or "to get." In some cases both may be appropriate. Explain your choices.

1. Environmental pollution _____ blamed for many birth defects.

2. Farley Mowat _____ recognized wherever he goes.

3. A fox _____ hurt by the steel trap.

4. A biosphere _____ built to study the effects of acid rain.

5. Jason _____ hit by a bolt of lightning.

Note: The verb "be" is always possible, but "get" is only possible in informal situations.

One Step Beyond — Create an Activity

Exercise F

Create ten sentences in the passive voice that describe the location, origin, or purpose of various things. Write these sentences on a piece of paper, leaving a blank line for the subject item. Exchange your exercise with a classmate and try to identify the missing things.

EXAMPLE: _____ was invented by Alexander Graham Bell.

The telephone was invented by Alexander Graham Bell.

Exercise G

Write a paragraph for potential visitors to your native country, warning them about one type of severe weather condition that frequently occurs. Describe the weather condition and what should be done if it occurs. Use both passive and active voices, as well as vocabulary from the unit. Then rewrite the paragraph as a fill-in-the-blank activity. Replace each verb with a blank followed by the base form of the verb in brackets [ ]. Also replace all the weather-related words with blanks, followed by the word scrambled and in parentheses ( ). Exchange your exercise with a partner.

EXAMPLE: In Southwestern Ontario, _____ (nneful) clouds race across the land destroying everything in their path. Life-saving steps must _____ [take] if you see a _____ (ntoarod).

Prewriting is an essential part of the writing process; it allows you to get your ideas down so that you can look at them. Often, the most difficult aspect of writing is getting started. There are several prewriting steps that writers should routinely follow in order to produce better pieces of writing.

The Topic

One stumbling block facing many writers is how to get started when presented with a topic. You may not know how to narrow down the topic or how much you really know about that topic. In order to get the "creative juices flowing," it is essential to spend five to ten minutes doing a prewriting activity.

Prewriting

The following are three ways to generate ideas using brainstorming. The purpose of brainstorming is to generate an excess of ideas. From these ideas, you select the ones that help you focus on your topic, and discard those that do not support your topic. It is not necessary to use all three methods; after experimenting with each, you will find the one that works best for you.

1. Freewriting

For ten minutes, write as many ideas as you can think of about a topic. *Don't worry about spelling, grammar, or punctuation.* The purpose is to record free thoughts that you will sort out at a later point.

EXAMPLE: Topic — Devastating Floods

Manitoba witnessed some of the most devastating floods ever witnessed in that province. Millions of doolars in damages volunteers from all over came to help out. Many people donated clothes, blankets and non-perishable food items to help out the flood victims — the red Cross was overwelmed wioth the donations. Many people couldn't return to their homes for several weeks and had no idea how damafged their homes would be when they returned. Animals and pets were sometimes left sttranded in the fast exedus — volunteers in boats captured animals and attempted to reunite with their owners. Military played a key role...

2. Cluster Map

Draw a circle in the middle of the page and write the name of your topic inside the circle. Then draw six to eight lines radiating from the circle like the spokes of a wheel. At the end of each line, draw another circle. Write words or phrases that relate to the topic in these secondary circles. From the secondary circles, draw radiating lines to another set of circles. Fill these new circles with words or phrases related to the words or phrases in each secondary circle.

EXAMPLE:

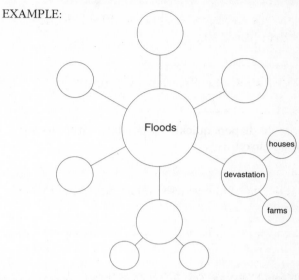

3. Star Map

Draw a six-pointed star and write the name of your topic inside the star. Label the points of the star with the question words: Who? What? When? Where? Why? How?. Consider the answers to each question as they relate to the topic and jot down this information beside each point of the star. (These are also known as the reporter's questions or W5H questions.)

EXAMPLE:

Who? farmers, townfolk, military, volunteers
What? flood relief, evacuation, tragedy, loss
When? March, 1997
Where? Manitoba, Minnesota
Why? rain, melting snow, high water levels, broken dams
How? act of nature, human struggles

Identify the Audience

It is very important to think about your audience before you start the writing process. Language and content will be influenced by the assumptions you make about the intended reader.

Narrowing the Topic

The topic you choose has to be sufficiently narrowed to be adequately developed in the length of the paragraph or essay you are required to write. If you were asked to write on the topic of **floods**, you could easily write about several aspects of floods such as recent floods, great historical floods, deaths due to floods, the tremendous costs of floods, etc. If you were asked to write only a paragraph, however, you would have to narrow the topic to encompass only one aspect of floods, for example, the **1997 flood in Manitoba**. This could still be too large a topic to deal with as the 1997 flood in Manitoba could encompass many aspects — for example, economic costs, the ruin of farmland, and the role of the army. Once you have selected **one** aspect of the topic, you can write your topic sentence.

The Topic Sentence

The topic sentence states the main idea of the paragraph; all other sentences in the paragraph must relate to the topic sentence. It is usually general in content in order to introduce all the ideas that follow. It must also express a controlling idea that indicates the writer's attitude towards the topic. It is usually the first sentence of the paragraph because it tells what the paragraph is about, but can also be positioned as the second or concluding sentence.

Exercise A

The following sentences are possible topic sentences for a paragraph about the **1997 floods in Manitoba**. Underline the controlling idea in each sentence.

1. The economic damage caused by the flood in Manitoba is still being calculated.

2. Farmers lost a lifetime of work as the 1997 Manitoba floods washed away their livelihood.

3. The army played a key role in the aftermath of the flood.

4. Volunteers came to help the flood victims in any way they could.

Note: Because the topic sentence is key to writing an effective paragraph, it should be a complete sentence (containing a subject and verb and expressing a complete thought) and limited in scope.

Exercise B

Place a checkmark beside the sentences below that make effective topic sentences.

☐ 1. We don't care about our environment.

☐ 2. Global warming poses a serious threat to our weather.

☐ 3. Global warming is a big problem.

☐ 4. Which means cars are major polluters.

☐ 5. The future of our planet is in our hands.

☐ 6. The environment

Exercise C

In the following paragraphs, underline the topic sentence that states the main idea of each paragraph.

1. Our lives are greatly influenced by the weather; it affects how we dress, how we feel, and what we do daily. As we step out our front door each day, we are subjected to nature's whims. Before venturing outdoors, we check the weather to ensure that we are dressed appropriately. A light jacket would offer no protection against the bitter cold winds in early winter, for example. In addition to influencing our choice of clothing, the weather also affects us physically. Many people suffering from physical ailments, such as arthritis, feel the discomfort of impending rain as it makes their joints ache. This may limit the activities they are able to partake in on those wet, rainy days. Physical discomfort is not the only way in which weather affects our daily activities. No one in their right mind would start out on a long drive during blizzard conditions. When the sun blazes and it becomes unbearably hot, we may be prisoners in our air-conditioned homes. The weather definitely influences our daily lives through how we dress, our state of health, and the activities we partake in.

2. First Nations peoples peacefully co-exist with nature. They believe that they should not take more from the land than they can use. Most fish and hunt to feed themselves, not for commercial exploitation. Moreover, they show their respect for the land by thanking the spirits for its use. The First Nations people's treatment of the land will ensure that it is still fruitful for future generations. Some other cultures have tried to conquer nature. Not content to take enough from the land for their own sustenance, they seek to make a commercial profit from it. The aim is to conquer, not co-exist. The result is a dying planet. The First Nations peoples have learned to live in harmony with nature, but many other cultures have not.

Exercise D

Write topic sentences for the following topics. Remember that the topic sentences must have a controlling idea and be limited in scope to ensure a coherent paragraph. Brainstorm your topic using the prewriting techniques previously outlined.

1. The environment

_____

_____

2. Native myths

_____

_____

3. Famous scientists

_____

_____

4. The origin of the planet

_____

_____

5. Nature's power

_____

_____

6. Natural disasters

_____

_____

☑ **Prewriting Checklist**

☐ Did I brainstorm ideas?

☐ Did I clearly identify the audience?

☐ Is my topic sufficiently narrowed?

☐ Is my topic sentence a complete sentence expressing a complete thought?

☐ Does my topic sentence introduce the topic?

☐ Does my topic sentence contain a controlling idea?

UNIT 2
Strange But True

Vocabulary 1

Exercise A

Complete the paragraph by filling in the blanks with appropriate words from the vocabulary list below.

astrology	numerology	telepathy
reincarnation	psychic	subconscious
clairvoyance		

Belief in (1) _____ phenomena is common throughout the world. Canadians are not the only ones, for example, who enjoy reading their horoscopes daily in the newspapers; many cultures believe in (2) _____ . The idea that the stars influence personalities and human behaviour in some way has existed for centuries. In fact, some cultures even believe in (3) _____ — the idea that numbers influence our luck. Incidents of (4) _____ and (5) _____ are frequently reported in the media. In one case, a father saved the life of his daughter who had fallen into a flooding river on the way home from school because he could "see in his mind" that his daughter was in danger. In another case, a woman in Halifax claimed she could communicate in thought with her sister in Ontario. The sisters appeared to have the ability to read each other's minds so that one sister could actually "tell" the other that she had fallen down a flight of stairs. Some argue that such incidents are simply physical cues planted in the (6) _____ mind. In other words, we read cues from the physical world and store them in our minds without being aware of them consciously. (7) _____ is perhaps one of the most commonly held beliefs. The very notion that our existence ceases at death is very difficult to comprehend. Not only do some people believe in a life "somewhere else" after our earthly death, many believe that we actually come back to earth as a new life form — a person, an animal, or even a plant. Unfortunately, it is very difficult to confirm the existence of paranormal events scientifically. That is why, despite our belief in the supernatural, it remains just that — a belief, not a fact.

Exercise B

Complete the crossword by filling in the blanks using the words below.

psychokinetic	curse	medium
poltergeist	shaman	omens
voodoo	apparitions	telepathy
seance	premonitions	levitate

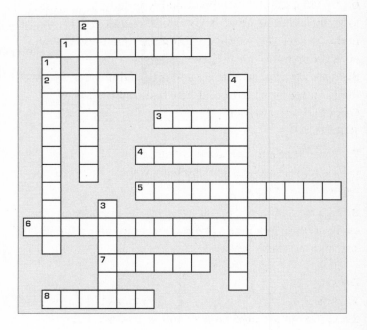

Across

1. A Polish medium called Stanislawa Tomczyk could _____ small objects between her hands, such as small balls and cigarettes. It looked as if she was controlling them by threads as if they were puppets. On one occasion, a teaspoon threw itself out of a glass after she had concentrated on it.

2. The Romans were very superstitious. Many emperors had personal astrologers who advised them when making decisions. There were also priests and priestesses who interpreted _____ from the gods.

3. A 12th-century writer called Giraldus Cambrensis wrote about a _____ put upon the inhabitants of the region of Ossary in Ireland in the 6th century. Every seven years, two people from the region had to become wolves. If they survived, they were allowed to return to their old lives, and two more people had to take their places.

4. The native religion of Haiti, _____ , is centred around ceremonies in which the worshippers are taken possession of by spirits.

5. Those who practise spirit religions often claim to be able to summon up _____ of demons, spirits, and even animals. One witness to an African ceremony, Harry Wright, described how a young girl danced a "leopard dance" by firelight. As she danced, Wright could see shadows all around her which his companion said were clearly leopards. At the high point of the dance, three real leopards suddenly appeared, walked across the clearing, and disappeared back into the jungle. It was as if they had come to investigate the phantom leopards called up by the dance.

6. In 1983, Carol Compton, a nanny in Italy, was brought to court and accused of deliberately starting fires in the homes where she worked. During the trial, however, it emerged that the fires behaved oddly — one did not burn the spot where it started, for instance, although surrounding furniture was charred. It was believed by many that Carol had unconscious _____ ability to start fires.

7. While trying to contact the dead, the _____ goes into a trance and the spirits may show their presence by moving the table.

8. In a typical _____ , people sit in a circle and touch hands to help concentration (and to make sure that no one cheats!).

Down

1. Was a _____ responsible for moving the coffins in a sealed family vault in Barbados? Between 1807 and 1820, every time the vault was opened to bring in another coffin, the place was found in disarray. The coffins lay at all angles, and sometimes stood upright as if they had been flung across the chamber.

2. _____ is difficult to control as it needs the participation of two or more people — one actively trying to transmit his or her thoughts, and the other trying to receive and understand them.

3. Tribal _____ have to go through rigorous initiation rites before they can begin practising.

4. Sometimes accidents are avoided through _____ . One man, while on holiday in Scotland, sent his daughter out for a walk. Suddenly, he "knew" that she was in danger, and sent a servant who found her going to the beach to sit on some stones by a railway bridge. Later, they heard that an engine fell off the bridge and onto the stones at the time she would have been there.

One Step Beyond — Create An Activity
Exercise C

Write a short paragraph in pencil about the supernatural, using at least three of the words from Exercises A and B. Erase the three vocabulary words and exchange your paper with a classmate. Can your classmate fill in the blanks with the correct words?

Vocabulary 2 Expansion

Exercise A

Read the following sentences to determine the meanings of the prefixes. Write the meaning of the words and the prefix.

1. a) During hypnosis, the psychiatrist instructed the patient that when she awoke she would no longer believe in ghosts. As a result of this posthypnotic suggestion, the patient was cured of her fear of ghosts.

   b) The work of many great artists, including Vincent Van Gogh, was not recognized during their lifetime, but rather posthumously.

   posthypnotic _____

   posthumously _____

   post- _____

2. a) Scientists have attempted to provide scientific explanations for many paranormal occurrences in an effort to demystify the supernatural.

   b) Classifying shaman as magicians demeans their role as healers and spiritual leaders.

   demystify _____

   demean _____

   de- _____

3. a) In an out-of-body experience, the body transcends the physical world.

    b) Spirits sometimes transmit messages to others through mediums.

    transcend _____

    transmit _____

    trans- _____

4. a) Monotheistic cultures believe in only one god; there are other cultures, however, that believe in several gods.

    b) The belief in the supernatural may be just an interesting pursuit in an otherwise monotonous existence.

    monotheistic _____

    monotonous _____

    mono- _____

5. a) The woman was dissatisfied with the explanation that her premonition about the plane crash was coincidental.

    b) The television psychic was discredited when it was revealed that 90% of his predictions failed to come true.

    dissatisfied _____

    discredited _____

    dis- _____

6. a) A curse is also known as a malediction because when someone puts a curse on you that person speaks a word or sentence asking for something bad to happen to you.

    b) Not all ghosts are malicious; some are well-meaning and pleasant.

    malediction _____

    malicious _____

    mal- _____

Exercise B

Some prefixes have more than one meaning. Using the meanings given in the answer key for Exercise A, brainstorm as many words as you can for each prefix. Then choose two words from the list for each prefix and create two sentences using these words.

Exercise C - Wordbuilding

Use the prefixes presented in this unit (Student Book and Workbook) to build words. Attach appropriate prefixes to the words below. Use a dictionary to confirm that the words you choose are appropriate. Write them on a separate sheet.

Prefixes					
pre-	*super-*	*re-*	*tele-*	*sub-*	*para-*
post-	*de-*	*trans-*	*mono-*	*dis-*	*mal-*

Words		
arrange	human	gram
mature	secondary	reputable
view	nova	marketing
mission	heading	figure
psychology	script	caffeinated
code	port	honest
formed	plant	agree
adjusted	phrase	

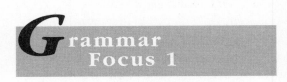

Grammar Focus 1

REPORTED SPEECH (STATEMENTS)

Exercise A

Report what these politicians said.

1. Ms. H.: A few ghosts from my past have come back to haunt me.

    Ms. H. admitted _____

    _____

2. Mr. B.: There were many unexplained events in this government last year.

    Mr. B. said _____

    _____

3. Mr. J.: I believe that the leader was a fox in his previous life.

    Mr. J. was overheard saying _____

    _____

4. Mr. M.: I predict that my party will balance the budget this year.

    Mr. M. predicted _____

    _____

5. Mr. P.: I am learning to speak a second language because I have discovered that being unilingual in a bilingual country is a curse.

Mr. P. assured voters _____

_____

6. Mr. J.: I envision a country my children and grandchildren can be proud of.

Mr. J. announced _____

_____

7. Mr. L.: One doesn't have to be a psychic to know that governing a bilingual country will continue to be a challenge in the future.

Mr. L. said _____

_____

Exercise B

Identify the reported speech in this news report from the weekly tabloid, *Star Gazing*, and quote what the speakers must have said.

Yesterday the Academy of Space Science announced that a possible UFO had been sighted by one of its senior research scientists at its California observatory. Jerome Harrold, Executive Director of the Academy, said that Dr. Marilyn Boch had reported seeing a spaceship-like object at about 10:15 p.m. on Tuesday night. Dr. Boch immediately began to take pictures of the unusual object with one of the observatory's telescopic cameras. Mr. Harrold admitted that he was sceptical about the sighting despite the photographs. When interviewed later, Dr. Boch confirmed that she had been working in the Academy's observatory when she saw a gold, oval-shaped flying machine racing through the night sky. According to Dr. Boch, sightings of this nature are quite common but rarely reported.

The senior scientist acknowledged that other scientists had also seen UFOs but had not reported them because they didn't want to jeopardize their reputations. She admitted that the government was putting pressure on the scientific community to withhold information about UFO sightings in order to avoid mass panic.

Harrold denied this and suggested that perhaps Dr. Boch had been watching too many episodes of *The X-Files*. He assured *Star Gazing* that the Academy would hold a complete investigation into the sighting.

What did they say to the reporter?

Jerome Harrold: _____

Jerome Harrold: _____

_____

Jerome Harrold: _____

_____

Jerome Harrold: _____

Dr. Marilyn Boch: _____

_____

Dr. Marilyn Boch: _____

_____

Dr. Marilyn Boch: _____

_____

Dr. Marilyn Boch: _____

_____

*G*rammar Focus 2

REPORTED SPEECH (QUESTIONS)

Exercise A — A reported interview

A graduate psychology student interviewed Noel about his beliefs and experiences with the paranormal. Based on the reported answers of Noel, create the questions the interviewer might have asked.

EXAMPLE: *Reported response:* Noel said he did believe in the supernatural.

Reported question: The interviewer asked Noel if he believed in the supernatural.

1. Noel said he read his horoscope about once a week.

The interviewer asked Noel _____

_____

_____

2. Noel replied that he had had paranormal experiences.

The interviewer asked Noel _____

_____

_____

3. Noel said he had experienced about ten supernatural phenomena in his life.

The interviewer asked Noel _____

_____

4. Noel answered that he didn't know what "psychokinesis" was.

The interviewer asked Noel _____

_____

5. Noel said that his most recent paranormal experience happened about a year ago.

The interviewer asked Noel _____

_____

_____

6. Noel stated that he doesn't think he is psychic.

The interviewer asked Noel _____

_____

_____

7. Noel said that he would consider participating in an experiment involving levitation.

The interviewer asked Noel _____

_____

_____

8. Noel agreed that he would call the interviewer's office to confirm the time of the experiment.

The interviewer asked Noel _____

_____

_____

Grammar in Use

Exercise B — Reported Speech (Statements and Questions)

Read "A Cradle of Love," which is a true account of an experience with the supernatural, and then answer the following questions using reported speech.

1. What did the boy on the terrace shout to Daniel as he arrived for the party?

_____

_____

2. What did Daniel's friends ask him after he had fallen through the skylight?

_____

_____

3. What did José's mother tell Daniel as she hugged him?

_____

_____

A Cradle of Love

Eight-year-old Daniel lived in Buenos Aires, a huge city in Argentina, South America. Here, the architecture is very mixed, with high apartment buildings like towers next to two-story buildings, and low houses all around. Today was the day Daniel was going to attend his friend José's birthday party. He was very excited for children here, as everywhere, love parties!

José lived just two blocks away from Daniel. The two always walked to school together, and Daniel had often played on the big terrace in the back of José's house. From the terrace, the boys could see the roofs of surrounding houses. A wall separated them from the building next door.

That afternoon, Daniel walked to José's house, carrying a birthday present for him. Several boys were already on the terrace. "Hey, Daniel!" one shouted. "You're just in time to play ball."

Daniel joined his pals, and the boys threw the ball around. All of a sudden someone missed a catch, and the ball sailed over the wall onto the roof of the building next door. Instantly, the boys climbed up the wall and scrambled onto the roof.

"There's the ball!" Daniel saw it first, lying on top of a glass skylight. Daniel had seen such skylights before, on top of his school's roof. Skylights save energy by letting sun inside, and Daniel knew the glass they used was very hard. This large pane would hold an eight-year-old boy easily. Daniel stepped up onto the skylight, reached for the ball, and...

Crash! The window shattered into a million pieces. Daniel fell through it, and hurtled toward the basement floor below.

His fall seemed to take hours. Feeling as if he were in slow motion, Daniel spun upside down and around, completely out of control. Finally, he landed.

But... although he had fallen more than two stories, he seemed to be fine. Gingerly, Daniel felt his head, arms, and legs. Nothing was broken. He sat up. In spite of all the jagged glass surrounding him, he could see only one small cut on his right arm. It didn't even hurt. *Nothing* hurt.

"Daniel? Are you all right?" His friends were shouting down from the top of the roof near the skylight.

4. What did José's father say about Daniel's "lucky" fall?

_____

_____

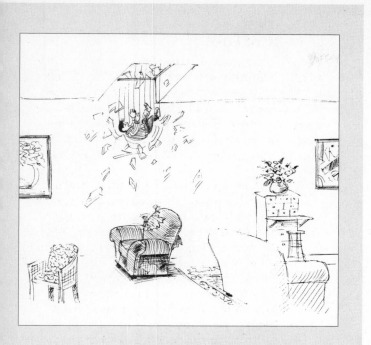

"I think so," he called back. He slowly got to his feet, grateful but confused. Soon he heard a key turn in a door and José's parents came running in to find him.

José's mother gave him a big hug. "The people who live in this house are on vacation," she explained. "They left their key with us."

José's father was looking around. "Daniel must have landed on this chair," he said. "That's what broke his fall."

Daniel turned around. There was an old ugly armchair behind him, tilting because of a broken leg. He *had* landed on it before hitting the floor; now he remembered.

But something was very odd. Daniel realized he was in a luxurious living room, beautifully furnished. Why would such an old chair be in a room like this? Especially right underneath a skylight — as if it had been placed there just for him?

No one, not even the owners of the house, ever discovered who owned the chair, or where it had come from. "I thought it was a great coincidence at first," Daniel says. "But now I believe my guardian angel moved that chair from somewhere else, to save my life. He was watching out for me that day. And he still does."

5. What did Daniel conclude about how the old chair had got there?

_____

_____

Exercise C

You overheard the following conversation yesterday evening at a restaurant. Report the conversation to a friend.

Jost: Hi. How did your day go?

Sandy: You wouldn't believe what happened to me today. I had the most bizarre experience. I mean, it was freaky.

Jost: You're kidding! What happened?

Sandy: After I took the kids to school this morning, I was driving along Main Street and when I stopped at the traffic light, I saw a ghost. I mean, I saw this apparition... this ghost-like figure heading towards my car. I couldn't tell if it was a man or a woman, but it seemed to be a young person.

Jost: Are you serious? Come on Sandy, you're putting me on — right?

Sandy: I'm not kidding you. I know it sounds crazy, but it's true. This "thing" came towards my car and I opened the side window.

Jost: You did what? Weren't you afraid? Why didn't you run it over?

Sandy: Run over a ghost, Jost? Besides, I wasn't afraid.

Jost: This is just too bizarre. I don't believe you.

Sandy: It gets better. So I rolled down my window and it says, "Help me! Help me! I'm dying!" At this point I thought I was going crazy, but I wasn't afraid. And then all of a sudden it disappeared. As the light changed, I drove on and just at the next corner I turned my head for some reason and I saw that there was some construction on one of the side streets. For some inexplicable reason, I felt drawn to the site. I just had this sense that I needed to pull over and check it out. The work crew wasn't there. There was a large hole in the ground that had been covered with boards, but a few of the boards were broken. I looked down and even though it was dark, I could see a body. It wasn't moving. The person was clearly unconscious.

Jost: Did you report this to the police?

Sandy: Of course. I ran to my cell phone and called the police immediately. An ambulance came and got the teen out. When I saw him, I recognized him as the apparition that had approached my car. They pronounced him dead on the scene and took him to the hospital. I told them what had happened to me and of course they didn't believe me. But I followed them to the hospital and half an hour later they told me he was alive, but in critical condition. Jost, he had come back to life. I know that this teen asked me to save his life, and I did.

Jost: You must be psychic or something.

Now report the conversation, using the following lines as your introduction:

Last night at a restaurant, I heard a woman telling her husband about a paranormal experience she had had. Her husband asked her...

_____

_____

_____

_____

_____

_____

_____

_____

_____

_____

_____

_____

_____

_____

Exercise D

Convert the quoted speech to reported speech and the reported speech to quoted speech.

1. "Stop this nonsense!" the father shouted to his son.

_____

_____

2. The shaman told him not to be afraid.

_____

_____

3. The clairvoyant told him to be careful.

_____

_____

4. "Get the camera!" she ordered her husband.

_____

_____

5. "Beware of a man with a blond beard," the medium warned the listeners.

_____

_____

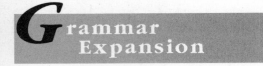

Grammar Expansion

Commands/Requests/Advice

In reported speech, commands are usually expressed by a command verb such as *tell*, *order*, and *command*. When expressing commands using these verbs, an object + infinitive must be used after the reporting verb.

EXAMPLE: *Quoted:* He said, "Leave me alone!"

Reported: He told <u>me</u> <u>to leave</u> him alone.
(object + infinitive)

When reporting a negative command, use object + *not* + infinitive.

EXAMPLE: *Quoted:* The medium announced (to the participants), "Don't delay."

Reported: The medium advised <u>the listeners</u> <u>not</u> to delay.
(object + *not* + infinitive)

Common Reporting Commands

advise	command	encourage
order	forbid	remind
recommend	warn	urge

One Step Beyond — Create An Activity

Exercise E

1. Use your imagination to write a dialogue between you and a friend who has just had a paranormal experience. Limit your writing to six exchanges each. Then exchange your dialogue with a partner and write your partner's dialogue in reported speech. Finally, work with your partner to edit each of your reported accounts.

2. Imagine that you have encountered one of the following supernatural *figures:* a fairy; a vampire; a witch; an apparition. Complete a police report. Report the details of the encounter and a detailed description of the *figure*. Exchange reports with a partner (police artist), who will use it to sketch the *figure*.

Writing

The Narrative Paragraph

The narrative paragraph tells a story which explains something. You may want to explain a strange but true experience that happened to you. In this case, you would include important details such as who was involved, what happened, and where, when, why, and how it happened.

An effective narrative paragraph:

1. ...has a clear purpose (it makes a point).
2. ...includes only those aspects and details that are relevant to your point.
3. ...is arranged in chronological order.
4. ...uses transitions to signal relationships, especially time relationships.
5. ...uses precise words to paint a written picture of the story.

Common narratives that most people are familiar with are the bedtime stories that we read to our children. Soap operas are another form of the narrative.

Exercise A

The sentences below were reported by someone who had a paranormal experience. They are not in the correct order. Reconstruct the narrative paragraph by putting the sentences in the correct sequence. Indicate the sequence by numbering each sentence in the answer box provided.

☐ After trying to contact my great-grandfather for about 45 minutes, we were about to give up when all of a sudden the table moved. It levitated about 10 centimetres above the ground. I was astonished.

☐ It was on a Sunday evening and we were sitting around the kitchen table in the dark, holding hands.

☐ I had attended the seance because I wanted to disprove my aunt's claims.

☐ Until that day, I had never had a supernatural experience and was very sceptical. Not only did great-grandfather levitate the table, he also spoke to us through my aunt, and eventually presented himself.

☐ It was three years ago, and I was attending a seance conducted by my aunt.

☐ I was told that my aunt had acute psychic powers, and had been a medium for my paternal great-grandfather for many years.

☐ Through these encounters, I have come to understand that there is much more to the world than meets the eye.

☐ My two sisters, my mother, and my uncle were also present.

☐ I vividly recall my first encounter with the ghost of my great-grandfather.

☐ Since that first encounter, my great-grandfather's ghost has presented itself to me many times, giving me useful advice and comforting me when I needed comfort.

Exercise B

Imagine you are Daniel in the story "A Cradle of Love." Write a narrative paragraph describing what happened to you when you were eight years old. Use the Narrative Paragraph Checklist at the end of this unit to edit your work.

Exercise C

Tell the story illustrated on the previous page in a narrative paragraph. Use the Narrative Paragraph Checklist at the end of this unit to edit your work. Write your story using one of the following openers.

a) I once attended a seance...
b) Last month my aunt was conducting a seance at her house...
c) My spouse and I went to a seance last week...
d) I love being a ghost...

Editing

Exercise D

There are 8 grammatical errors in the paragraph below. Find the errors and then write the corrections above the lines.

What I remember most about my arrival in this country was a feeling of hope. We arrived early one ice-cold winter morning in February. My mother and father were very exhausted, having travelled for so long with four young children. I was ten. When we stepped off the plane and looked around us at the grey, icy terminal buildings, my father said that he is not sure he will be able to live here. My mother took his hand and told him not to judge a whole country on its international airport. Still, my father insisted he can feel heaviness in her bones. "We would struggle here," he said. We children were very excited despite our lack of sleep and sadness at having left behind friends and relations. But on the walk from the plane to the terminal I felt a deep, cold chill creeping through my thin sweater. I began to feel tired, very tired, and at that moment I cursed under my breath that perhaps my father will be right. Perhaps we had made a mistake. My mother must have guessed my thoughts for she

hugged me warmly and, looking into my innocent eyes, soothed me, saying that our arrival has been a blessing. With tears in my eyes, I looked up at her face. As I glanced beyond her shoulders, a faint but steady ray of sunshine was creeping through a crack in the thick winter clouds. It felt warm and soothing. I recognized it as an omen, and, as the weak sun bathed my face, I knew that she was right. Our arrival would be a blessing. Taking my father's hand, I walked towards the terminal building with a sense of renewed hope.

Exercise E

Write a narrative paragraph about your arrival in a new country. Use the Narrative Paragraph Checklist below to edit your work.

☑ Narrative Paragraph Checklist

☐ Have I considered my audience and my purpose?

☐ Have I narrowed my topic?

☐ Did I brainstorm to generate ideas?

☐ Does my topic sentence tell the main point of my story?

☐ Have I chosen only the important events that relate to the main point of my topic sentence?

☐ Have I chosen details that clearly relate to my main point?

☐ Do the events in my paragraph follow a chronological order?

☐ Have I used transitional expressions to show the time order?

☐ Have I checked my paragraph to make sure that the meaning of each sentence is clear?

☐ Have I checked my paragraph to make sure that I have used precise words and the correct form of words?

☐ Have I proofread my paragraph for errors in grammar, punctuation, and spelling?

UNIT 3
The Road Less Travelled

Grammar Focus 1

ADJECTIVE ORDER

Exercise A

Categorize the adjectives in the five sentences below according to the descriptors in the chart. Note that not all categories are contained in every sentence.

EXAMPLE: Many medium-sized, ancient stone figures are found in Korea.

1. They found a single, small, intricately-carved black onyx fertility statue.
2. She described the "Three Sisters" in Australia's Blue Mountains as three colossal, majestic, pointy blue-hazed peaks.
3. Hundreds of small, pristine, crystal-clear lakes make it a perfect vacation destination.
4. Countless interesting, rust-coloured Aboriginal religious drawings cover the base of Ayers Rock.
5. Their large, formerly-grand, ancient dome-shaped temples dot the landscape.

Grandfather stones in Korea.

CATEGORY	DETERMINER	SIZE	GENERAL DESCRIPTION	AGE	SHAPE	COLOUR	MATERIAL	ORIGIN	PURPOSE
EXAMPLE	many	medium-sized		ancient			stone		
1									
2									
3									
4									
5									

Exercise B

Complete the following paragraph by writing the adjectives in parentheses in the appropriate order in the spaces provided.

New Zealand is the ideal destination for the
(1) _____ (adventurous nature) lover. The Routeburn Trail, located on the northern perimeter of the South Island, is a
(2) _____ (scenic, moderately-long) hike for young and old alike who wish to enjoy the breathtaking views that nature presents. (3) _____
_____ (curving, man-made, narrow) paths snake through dense areas of forest. Periodic (4) _____ (natural, small) clearings provide a welcome rest stop to drop
(5) _____ (heavy, waterproof) backpacks, sit back, and listen to the
(6) _____ (unusual, countless) noises from birds and animals in the surrounding foliage. The trail winds its way to the
(7) _____ (sandy, white, vast) beach on several occasions, allowing the weary hiker to dip tired toes in the refreshing ocean. And just when exhaustion is setting in, there is a
(8)_____ (large, wood, ten-year-old) cabin where hikers can spend a dry, rejuvenating night before setting off on another day's journey.

Exercise C

Write phrases to describe the objects shown in the photographs.

2. teepee

_____

_____

3. kayak

_____

_____

4. doll

_____

_____

1. Native mask

_____

_____

5. dress

_____

_____

Grammar In Use
Exercise D

Advertisements are full of descriptive phrases enticing us to purchase products or services. Read the following descriptions and try to identify the product being sold.

1. "floating twin blades flex to fit your curves"

   _____

2. "it's all-beef, nutritious and used by top breeders throughout the country" _____

3. "smooth, creamy and calorie-reduced — perfect for those hot days" _____

4. "quickly cuts through the grease to leave a sparkling shine" _____

5. "a light, refreshing, quenching taste" _____

6. "colourfast, washable, drip-dry" _____

7. "coated non-stick surface needs no oil"

   _____

8. "it leaves your skin feeling clean and soft"

   _____

9. "top-quality — one coat is guaranteed to cover in a single application" _____

10. "it's so lifelike it cries and wets its diaper"

   _____

One Step Beyond – Create An Activity
Exercise E

Write five product descriptions and see if your classmates can identify the products.

Exercise F

Your team of three or four is made up of promotion coordinators representing several fabulous resorts. In your promotional magazine, you want to describe the different resort destinations vividly in order to attract clientele. Your team will write four detailed descriptions for the following types of resorts:

1. Relaxing
2. Fun For the Whole Family
3. Exciting
4. Educational

Put your vacation getaway descriptions together to form a travel brochure. Copy the brochure for the other teams. Each class member will select the vacation that most appeals to him or her based on the descriptions provided.

Vocabulary 1
Exercise A

Underline the synonyms or expressions in the paragraph below that have the same meaning as the following words. Write the word above the underlined portion.

bravely	adventurous	dedicated
courage	inspire	persevere

Women travellers have historically been underrepresented in our history books, yet their accomplishments stimulate countless women to challenge their perceived borders. Women who refuse to give up have traipsed into foreign countries, without fear, to explore the unknown. These women, who are willing to take risks in order to experience new situations, are devoted to expanding their personal horizons. In societies that have traditionally sheltered and protected women, it is only those women who are full of bravery that take the initiative to follow their dreams.

Exercise B

Complete the following chart with the various parts of speech. Note that it may not be possible to form every part of speech in every case. Then write a sentence for each word that demonstrates its meaning.

Noun	Verb	Adjective	Adverb
			bravely
		adventurous	
		dedicated	
		courageous	
	inspire		
	persevere		

Exercise C

Replace the italicized words in the following sentences with more precise descriptive words.

1. Toronto is a very *large, beautiful* city._____

   _____

2. I thought that the Sydney Opera House was a *beautiful* building._____

   _____

3. The food in Spain was *good.*_____

   _____

4. The people in Thailand were *nice.* _____

   _____

5. I saw ivory carvings in a Taiwanese museum that were *small and beautiful.* _____

   _____

6. The Indonesian dancers were *good.* _____

   _____

7. Her father is *nice-looking.* _____

   _____

8. The plane trip was *okay.* _____

   _____

9. The mountain water was *cold.*_____

   _____

10. France was *interesting.*_____

    _____

Vocabulary Expansion

Descriptions are often made vivid by comparing the unknown to something with which the reader might be familiar. The degree of similarity can be emphasized using adverbs that intensify the adjective or adverb (intensifiers).

EXAMPLE: Australia is **considerably** larger than New Zealand.

Other useful expressions are:

small difference   a bit
                         slightly
                         somewhat
                         much
                         substantially
large difference   considerably

Exercise D

Compare the following subjects using an intensifier.

1. Switzerland / Mexico

   _____

2. Thai food / Indonesian food

   _____

3. Japanese bullet train / express train

   _____

4. First class / economy airline seats

   _____

5. temperature in southern Colombia / temperature in Ecuador

   _____

Grammar Focus 2

RELATIVE CLAUSES

Exercise A

Fill in the blanks with an appropriate relative pronoun. More than one answer may be possible.

Gloria had just graduated from university when she decided to take some time to explore exotic parts of the world (1) _____ she was unfamiliar with. Her first stop was Australia, (2) _____ is known for its koala bears and kangaroos. She travelled around Australia with some Brits (3) _____ she had met on the plane. Together they travelled up the coast to Queensland. There, on the Great Barrier Reef, (4) _____ is the largest living organism in the world, they learned to scuba dive. She still has fond memories of hitchhiking up the coast to Kakadu National Park, (5) _____ is home to incredible wildlife. Her next stop was New Zealand, (6) _____ is made up of three main islands. Each island has its own unique characteristics. New Zealanders and tourists (7) _____ love to go hiking have many excellent trails to choose from. Gloria managed to make it through a couple of tough but spectacular trails. From there it was on to Southeast Asia —

that was a whole new ball game!

Note: Traditionally, it was not acceptable to end a sentence
with a preposition as in the first sentence of this paragraph.
In formal writing it is still not acceptable; however, in
informal writing it is quite common.

Exercise B

Combine the following sentences using relative clauses.
Remember to use appropriate punctuation if the clause is
non-restrictive.

1. Barb flew to Thailand. She had never been out of
    Canada.

    _____

    _____

2. She met her sister there. Her sister had been living in
    Japan.

    _____

    _____

3. They enjoyed the food. It was hot and spicy.

    _____

    _____

4. They slept in guest houses. They were clean, cheap,
    and comfortable.

    _____

    _____

5. She bought a beautiful tapestry in the market at a good
    price. She had haggled over the price.

    _____

    _____

6. Barb rode an elephant while trekking in northern
    Thailand. The elephant could carry two people.

    _____

    _____

7. The sisters had a great time. They had a lot of catching
    up to do.

    _____

    _____

8. They saw some traditional dancers. They were very
    skilled and graceful.

    _____

    _____

9. The temples were awe-inspiring. The temples were
    extremely ornate.

    _____

    _____

10. It was a great experience. She will probably never
    have the opportunity to repeat it.

    _____

    _____

Exercise C

Complete the following sentences about your travel
habits.

1. I am someone who

    _____

    _____

2. I enjoy visiting places that

    _____

    _____

3. I like to try foods which

    _____

    _____

4. I don't enjoy seeing children who

    _____

    _____

5. The only country that

    _____

    _____

6. I take photographs that

    _____

    _____

7. I try to find locations where

    _____

    _____

8. I would never spend summertime in a country
    where

    _____

    _____

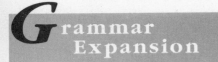

Grammar Expansion

Relative pronouns can be eliminated from sentences if the pronoun functions as an object in the sentence, or if the main verb or auxiliary in the relative clause is *be*.

EXAMPLES: The pen pal **that** I wrote to for the last ten years is coming to visit me.

The pen pal I wrote to for the last ten years is coming to visit me.

The girl **who is** watching TV is my sister.

The girl watching TV is my sister.

Exercise D

Cross out the relative pronouns or relative pronouns + *be* in the following sentences if possible. Be prepared to explain why you chose to eliminate them.

1. Have you seen the movie that Steven Spielberg made?
2. I am the person whom the lyrics are referring to.
3. Anyone who has ever seen the movie will agree.
4. Everyone who is invited is expected to attend.
5. The boy that I borrowed the pen from is absent today.
6. I saw a movie that you are sure to like.
7. It is the smell of fresh paint which gives her a headache.
8. I saw the band which you told me about last weekend.

Exercise E

The following article details the experiences of some modern-day explorers and is written by one of the participants, John Dunn.

Underline at least five relative clauses in this passage. Write an R above the clause if it is restrictive and NR above the clause if it is non-restrictive. Draw a circle around the noun being modified.

Traversing Baffin Island

My desire to traverse Baffin Island had nothing to do with turning 40 the day before I set out. No, it came from half a lifetime of dreaming about this untrammeled wilderness in northern Canada, one so

5 enormous that it would take six months to trek its length.

As a young man in England, where the manicured countryside was the opposite of everything I imagined as wild, I'd studied maps of

10 North America, searching for places where there were no roads, towns or railways. Later, between jobs as a geologist in the Australian outback, I travelled by boat up the west coast of Greenland and made ski trips across Ellesmere Island, Devon

15 Island, and northern Labrador, learning to live out on the land. Yet Baffin still beckoned.

As our plane touched down on Baffin's northern Brodeur Peninsula on March 27, 1994, I saw polar bear tracks crisscrossing the snow. Thirty hours out

20 of my house in Calgary, Alberta, and I'd already dropped a notch on the food chain. "Better keep an eye out," Mike Sharp said. Mike, Bob Saunders, and I would ski the first five-week leg to Pond Inlet. Later Sandy Briggs, Graeme Magor, and Glen Cowper

25 would join the expedition for varying periods.

Back home, as I was planning the route, I'd marveled at the fjords that carved into Baffin's northeastern coast and wondered at the jigsaw puzzle of land and water that straddles the island's mid-

30 section. Now it was time to see what was out there.

Loading gear onto my sled, I stepped into my skis and followed Mike and Bob across the sea ice.

"It feels completely unnatural to ski across open water," Sandy Briggs says of his slosh across Home Bay. Despite being soaked for hours, his feet stay tolerably warm, thanks to the insulating effect of water trapped in his boots.

Taking advantage of a gusty morning, Bob hops on his sled for a spin across the slick ice — a run made more exciting by the sail blocking his view. We normally ski in front of our sleds, using the sails to provide a helpful push.

With a knack for building shelters out of snow, Sandy constructs an outhouse on an ice field south of Pond Inlet. Other team members prefer simply to walk down the trail. Returning from one such trip on a day when a blizzard confined us to our tents, Bob checks the sleds and reports that an arctic fox has been chewing on the runaway straps of his skis.

Mike peers out of the tent. "That's not a fox," he says. "That's a polar bear cub!"

Eager to avoid a confrontation with its mother, who may be nearby, we shoo the cub away with noisemakers.

Facing temperatures as low as minus 42° F [–41° C], which turns Mike's beard a frosty white, we spend most of the first few weeks on Baffin just trying to keep warm. The arduous work requires 5500 calories a day, including lots of cheese and margarine.

Heading toward warmer land, Mike crosses Okoa Bay in late June. Shallow ribbons of meltwater braid the surface of the thick ice before draining down cracks or seal holes into the ocean below.

Trading sleds for folding kayaks, delivered to us by a floatplane, we step off the Penny Ice Cap directly into summer. For the next two months, we paddle and portage through a maze of lakes and rivers, disassembling the kayaks when necessary to carry them over rough ground.

"They're not so bad if you keep moving," Sandy says of the mosquitoes that swarm around us as soon as we leave the ice cap in Auyuittuq National Park Reserve. Within weeks they are replaced by infuriating mobs of blackflies. For Sandy it's "all part of the fun of being here."

Heading inland from the east coast, we follow a traditional route of caribou hunters that has been used since the first people migrated to Baffin from Alaska some 3500 years ago. On a hillside above our tents near Amittok Lake, old *inuksuit*, or stone markers, recall the presence of earlier travellers.

On September 15, Bob and I start the final back-packing part of our journey. Within hours it begins to snow.

Resting in peace on a lonely beach on Isabella Bay, a grave marker recalls the fate of a harpooner from a 19th-century British whaling ship. His memorial reminds us that life in the north can be as fragile as an arctic poppy, a lesson Bob and I learn in late September.

Trudging up a hill above Jackman Sound, we surprise a polar bear sow as she lumbers out from behind a boulder with her cub. Glaring at us, she

huffs — signal of a possible attack. Fortunately she
turns and drops down the other side of the hill, cub
at her heels. For the rest of the journey we
announce our presence, banging on our cooking
pot and singing out warnings like devotees of some
mad sect.

A few days later Bob and I reach the southern
tip of the island, our final goal. What a privilege it
was to have travelled for 192 days on what Sandy
called our quest for wonder, gazing down on
cottony clouds above Gibbs Fjord, watching
glaucous gulls swoop past cliffs painted rust red
with lichens, or listening to the surreal tinkling of
rafts of candle ice shoved by storm waves against
the rocky shore of Nettiling Lake.

Months of intense but exhilarating physical exer-
tion and cold: A small price to pay for a lifetime of
memories.

Glossary

(1) *traverse* — cross

(4) *untrammeled* — wild, untouched

(8) *manicured* — well taken care of

(16) *beckoned* — called

(21) *notch* — level

(27) *fjords* — long strips of sea between steep hills

(29) *straddles* — runs on either side

(34) *slosh* — move through water

(38) *gusty* — windy

(58) *arduous* — difficult

(68) *portage* — carry the boat overland

Exercise F

Write descriptive sentences identifying the following.

EXAMPLE: Baffin Island

Baffin Island, which is located in northern Canada, is sparsely populated.

1. polar bear

_____

_____

2. the expedition

_____

_____

3. the temperature

_____

_____

4. kayaks

_____

_____

5. first people

_____

_____

6. southern tip of Baffin

_____

_____

7. memories

_____

_____

8. Bob Saunders

_____

_____

Vocabulary Expansion

Exercise A

Read the following fictional interview and try to determine the meaning of the idioms. Write a brief definition for each idiom.

Reporter:	You really put your life **on the line** to make this epic voyage. Was the potential danger part of the thrill?
Don Starkell:	My sons and I knew that we would face many challenges on our trip, but we were determined to **give it our best shot.**
Reporter:	Did you do much pre-trip preparation or had you decided just to **play it by ear?**
Don:	We knew we had to build up our muscle tone, endurance, not to mention finances. We did a lot of research concerning routes and weather conditions before we ventured out.
Reporter:	What were some of the biggest challenges you faced?
Don:	It would have to be the scorching heat and the bugs — you should have seen the size of some of them.
Reporter:	Did you ever consider quitting?
Don:	Well, there were times when we were literally **on our last legs**, but we always managed to bolster each other's spirits enough to get through it.
Reporter:	When you ran into trouble in the Amazon, I'm sure you really questioned your ability to persevere.
Don:	That's true, but we were so close to achieving our dream that we didn't want **to blow it** by giving up then.
Reporter:	Well Don, I have a lot of respect for you. I could certainly never have accomplished what you did, nor would I really have wanted to. You know what they say — **different strokes for different folks!**

1. on the line

    _____

2. give it one's best shot

    _____

3. play it by ear

    _____

4. on one's last legs

    _____

5. to blow it

    _____

6. different strokes for different folks

    _____

Exercise B

Complete the following sentences with the idioms from Exercise A. (You may need to change the pronoun.)

1. We aren't really sure where we are going on our vacation. We thought we'd just get in the car and

    _____ .

2. I know they say _____ , but do you honestly know anyone in his right mind who would pierce his tongue?

3. Despite an acute attack of stage fright, the actor went out and _____ .

4. The car is _____ . I'm not sure it will make it all the way to Florida.

5. The Prime Minister put his career _____ with his innovative election campaign in which he promised to quit his office if he didn't reduce the deficit to zero in three years.

6. This deal is crucial in determining if the company will stay afloat or go bankrupt, so please don't

    _____ .

Writing

The Descriptive Paragraph

The descriptive paragraph describes a person, event, object, feeling, or scene. The written words are like an artist's oils recreating a vision for others. What is described and the type of words used to evoke a vivid picture depend on the topic and purpose of the paragraph. Descriptive paragraphs are very common in travel literature, science reports, police reports, doctor's notes, etc.

An effective descriptive paragraph:

1. ...creates a vivid visual picture with words.
2. ...is arranged in a logical order (generally spatially).
3. ...includes only those aspects and details that support the controlling idea in the topic sentence.
4. ...uses vivid descriptive language that appeals to the senses to support the controlling idea in the topic sentence.
5. ...indicates the attitude of the writer towards the subject.
6. ...uses spatial transitional expressions to show place or position (at the top, under, to the left, on the right, beneath, next to, etc.)

Exercise A

When travelling, Marco loved to jot down vivid descriptions of places he visited on whatever scraps of paper he could find stuffed in his pockets. He wrote on napkins, ticket stubs — even toilet paper, when desperate. Help Marco write a paragraph describing the Sydney Opera House to submit to a popular travel magazine. Eliminate any sentences that do not support the topic sentence. You will have to supply some of your own information and transitional sentences.

Topic Sentence: The Sydney Opera House, which opened in 1974, is a prime example of splendid architecture set in a background of inner-city beauty.

Sydney is located in the state of New South Wales.

Behind the building, on the walkway, a band is busking for shelter money.

In front are the trendy cafés where a mosaic of people lounge around drinking their espressos.

To the right of the Opera House, you can see the magnificent botanical gardens with their exotic flora.

Framing the Opera House, slightly to the left, is the picturesque Sydney Harbour suspension bridge.

Opera music can be truly inspirational, although some say it is an acquired taste.

Australia is a former British penal colony.

The Opera House itself, with its unique curved designs, juts out into the harbour.

Exercise B

Use the following outline to write a paragraph describing the town of Banff.

To the left:	- the local pub - brightly painted - frequented by both locals and tourists
On the right:	- grocery store and drug store - there many years - friendly staff
Down the centre:	- stately streetlight standards - separate directions of traffic - romantic night atmosphere
At end of street:	- hotel resort - full of tourists - spectacular views
Behind the hotel:	- mountains - rising majestically - dwarf the hotel
Bottom of the mountain:	- stately pines - reach for the sky - dense
Middle of the mountain:	- scrub - sparse - brown

Mountain peak: - rocky
                    - distant

Exercise C

Imagine that you are John Dunn who wrote *Traversing Baffin Island.* You are writing to your spouse describing Bob Saunders to her. Use your imagination to create a complete picture.

Note: When describing a person, you may want to describe some or all of the following: facial appearance, body shape, fitness, mannerisms, habits, knowledge of the expedition, etc.

Editing

Exercise D

The following paragraph is very choppy and difficult to read because it contains too many short sentences and repeated words. Rewrite the paragraph, combining sentences with relative clauses where possible.

> The warm atmosphere created by Santa Fe's friendly, diverse people and rich traditions matches the warmth of the climate. Santa Fe's mosaic background is comprised of a variety of backgrounds. The predominant backgrounds come from Native Americans. Native Americans' ancestors have been in northern New Mexico for at least a thousand years. The strongest backgrounds also come from the descendants of the Spanish conquistadors. The Spanish conquistadors came north from Mexico in the 16th century. The two cultures share a love and respect for the land. The two cultures share a deep respect and love for the traditions that have been passed down from generation to generation. Santa Feans are friendly. Santa Feans have always been accepting of different cultures. As a consequence, people from all walks of life feel welcomed. Santa Fe is located in the desert. Santa Fe is very warm. Santa Fe is a great place to visit because of the people and the atmosphere.

Exercise E

Think about the most breathtaking scene you can remember when you wished you had a camera close at hand, but unfortunately did not. The only means you have of sharing your vision with anyone is through your detailed description. Write a paragraph describing the scene. Use the Descriptive Paragraph Checklist at the end of this unit to edit your work.

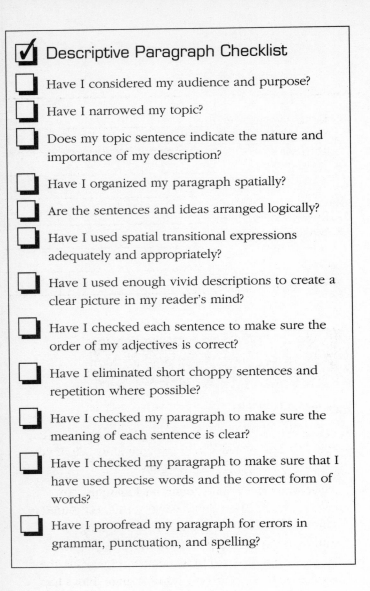

☑ Descriptive Paragraph Checklist

☐ Have I considered my audience and purpose?

☐ Have I narrowed my topic?

☐ Does my topic sentence indicate the nature and importance of my description?

☐ Have I organized my paragraph spatially?

☐ Are the sentences and ideas arranged logically?

☐ Have I used spatial transitional expressions adequately and appropriately?

☐ Have I used enough vivid descriptions to create a clear picture in my reader's mind?

☐ Have I checked each sentence to make sure the order of my adjectives is correct?

☐ Have I eliminated short choppy sentences and repetition where possible?

☐ Have I checked my paragraph to make sure the meaning of each sentence is clear?

☐ Have I checked my paragraph to make sure that I have used precise words and the correct form of words?

☐ Have I proofread my paragraph for errors in grammar, punctuation, and spelling?

UNIT 4
That's Not What I Meant

Vocabulary 1

Exercise A

Match all the definitions below to the correct idioms. One example has been done for you. Then create sentences for each idiom.

> to get someone to be precise
> to catch something
> to not understand
> to talk about something unrelated
> to get off topic
> to catch someone's drift
> to get off track
> to comprehend
> to not get the main idea
> to hear a rumour
> to force a comment
> to make someone tell something
> ~~to understand~~
> to avoid saying something directly
> to move away from the original topic
> to discover through gossip
> to not get to the point

Idioms   **Meanings**

a) to get the point of   _to understand_ _____
_____
_____
_____

b) to miss the point of _____
_____
_____
_____

c) to get sidetracked _____
_____
_____
_____

d) to beat around the bush _____
_____
_____
_____

e) to hear something through the grapevine _____
_____
_____
_____

f) to pin someone down on something _____
_____
_____
_____

Vocabulary Expansion

Exercise B

1. Read the paragraph below and guess the meaning of the five underlined idiomatic expressions. Or, if you wish, look them up in a dictionary.

Everyone loves a little gossip, including me. So when Maggie and I got together for tea last Saturday afternoon, I knew it was going to be a long afternoon. I had heard that our neighbours, the Kinders, had decided to move after 15 years in the building. There've been a lot of strange things happening next door recently — yelling, screaming, late night comings and goings. One night Mr. Kinder stormed out of the apartment and didn't return for three days. Anyway, their decision to move came about "very suddenly," and although I suspected they were about to break up, I couldn't be sure. Now Maggie has been a friend of the Kinders for a long time, so I knew that Maggie would have the scoop. At first, I wasn't sure how to <u>broach the subject</u>, but finally I commented that Mr. Kinder wasn't looking so well recently, and did Maggie know if he wasn't well. Well, she <u>rattled on for half an hour about</u> how Mrs. Kinder was a terrible wife, never doing anything around the house, and just demanding things all the time. They were breaking up and Mrs. Kinder would get what she deserved. I found it very curious that Maggie was so supportive of George Kinder and had nothing good to say about her friend, Mrs. Kinder, if you <u>catch my drift</u>. I guess only time will tell, but <u>mark my words</u>, no sooner will the Kinders have split than Maggie will be dating George. Of course, this is all speculation, so <u>mum's the word</u>.

2. Write a dialogue using at least three of the above expressions. Be prepared to perform the dialogue with a partner for your class.

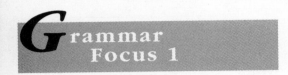

CONJUNCTIONS AND PREPOSITIONS OF CONTRAST

Exercise A

Fill in the blanks with the appropriate contrasting words/phrases from the list below. Use each word only once.

but	yet	although
even though	while	whereas
in spite of the fact that		despite

1. _____ Jasmine has been learning English for six years, she still has difficulty communicating with English speakers.

2. His words say he is not angry, _____ his gestures say he is.

3. _____ having attended the Effective Listening workshop at his company, Carlos remains a poor listener.

4. Maria doesn't believe she communicates well in English _____ many of her colleagues have commented on her good grasp of the language.

5. Ken is always trying to improve his communication skills _____ his wife makes no effort to improve her skills.

6. Professor Acker usually gets to the point quickly in her lectures _____ Professor Ramirez notoriously beats around the bush.

7. Manuela doesn't think she can write English very well _____ she can write a simple letter or short note.

One Step Beyond — Create An Activity

Exercise B

Write a sentence using each conjunction and preposition of contrast. Then rewrite each sentence, leaving out the expression of contrast. Exchange your activity with a classmate and fill in the blanks.

Exercise A

Each sentence below contains a word whose meaning is out of context. Underline the incorrect word and replace it with a form of one of the following words.

interact	barrier	feedback
interpersonal	gesture	perceive
vague	message	cue
concise		

1. Good business writing should not be wordy; it must be clear and challenging.

2. Although she had difficulty handling the tasks of the job, her photocopying skills were excellent; consequently, she was well liked by her colleagues.

3. Her poor listening skills remained a serious supervisor to her communication.

4. Ten minutes into his presentation, he noticed that people in the audience were beginning to fidget and make noise. Unfortunately, he didn't recognize that these were computers that people were losing interest in what he was saying.

5. The conversation became frustrating for Janet because Neil was very lazy about what he had expected. She wanted to pin him down on the specifics.

6. Steven enjoyed working for Soraya because she offered constructive paper clips about his work.

7. With a nod of her head, she wrote for him to stop talking.

8. Her training in group dynamics has made her a very inappropriate team player.

9. The success of this television talk show, in which viewers call the station to ask questions of celebrities, is attributed to its unfortunate format.

10. "I'm sorry, Mrs. Reiss isn't in at the moment. Would you like to leave a briefcase?"

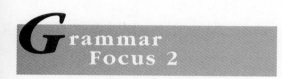

TRANSITION WORDS AND PHRASES OF CONTRAST

Exercise A

Use a transition word from the list below to join the contrastive ideas in the following sentences. Remember to use appropriate punctuation.

however	still	nevertheless
nonetheless	on the contrary	
even so	on the other hand	

1. Marjorie finds it difficult to confront people.

   She confronted her supervisor about an unacceptable comment.

   _____

   _____

2. John doesn't believe that criticizing the work of others is bad business practice.

   He believes constructive criticism is a good way to help people do their jobs better.

   _____

   _____

   _____

3. Dianne believes in constructive criticism.

   She condemns unproductive criticism.

   _____

   _____

   _____

4. Latin Americans often hug when saying hello.

   Germans usually shake hands.

   _____

   _____

   _____

5. People from countries such as Switzerland may appear reserved and aloof.

   They form close friendships with others.

   _____

   _____

   _____

6. Mr. Buhl has taught communications for three years.

   That doesn't mean he is an effective communicator himself.

   _____

   _____

   _____

7. Mrs. Lombardi believes in getting to the point.

   Sometimes she beats around the bush.

   _____

   _____

   _____

Exercise B —
Putting it all together

Read the following essay and then answer the questions.

Communication and Success in the Workplace

As I consider how effective my colleagues are in their jobs, I realize that our communication style greatly influences our success at work. Consider two employees, Elyse Meyers, Marketing Manager, and
5 Marybeth Armstrong, Accounting Manager, who work for the city tourist association. Elyse is an intelligent, well-educated woman dedicated to her work. She enjoys her work and supervises a staff of five. Marybeth is also intelligent and well-trained in
10 her profession. She too supervises a staff of five and enjoys her work. Their profiles seem similar, but whereas Elyse's staff are happy in their jobs and feel their supervisor is effective, Marybeth's staff complain that working for her is frustrating, and one
15 worker is even considering resigning. Of course, there could be many reasons for the differences in how the workers feel, but one marked difference between these two groups is the communication style of the department supervisors.
20   Both managers set a distinct tone when they began in their respective departments. When Elyse became manager five years ago, she began by meeting privately with everyone in her department — "to get acquainted," she said. Then she met with her
25 team as a group to set department goals and explain her expectations of the department. Elyse holds weekly department meetings religiously in which the team members update each other on what's happening in their areas. Once a year Elyse invites
30 her colleagues to a two-day staff retreat — a think-tank, where they all brainstorm new marketing initiatives and generally have a good time; while they work hard from 9 to 5, they do manage to make time for recreation and fun. When Marybeth joined
35 the company as manager three years ago, she was a bit unsure of how her colleagues would accept her age. She was quite a bit younger than some of her staff and, consequently, wanted to make sure that her staff respected her for her knowledge and skills.
40 She sent out a lengthy memo outlining her visions for the department and invited staff to see her personally if they wanted further clarification of her expectations. As a result of her impersonal communication style, she and her staff got off on the wrong
45 foot. Three years later she still hasn't developed the same rapport with the accounting department staff that Elyse enjoys with the marketing team. Marybeth writes a monthly update column for her department in the company newsletter which also keeps staff
50 informed about company initiatives. Even so, Marybeth's staff feel isolated and left in the dark about what is happening in the department. They complain that they aren't informed of department and company initiatives. Marybeth, in fact, is quite
55 annoyed that her staff are not more informed about

what's happening, considering that the information is available to them. Why the postscript on her column even invites any company staff member to contact her for more information.
60   Others in the company have begun to notice the differences in the two departments. Six months ago when the company president spoke to the two managers about the differences in their departments' performance, Marybeth responded that her staff
65 were simply not as motivated as the marketing people. "Besides," she claimed, "everyone knows that marketing people are outgoing while accountants are number crunchers, preferring to work alone with the details of numbers rather than with people".
70 Elyse, however, offered a different perspective and shared what she thought contributed to her team's success: effective communication. Marybeth quickly responded, confirming that she too communicates with her staff through her monthly updates in the
75 newsletter and her "open-door" policy. Although she agreed to look into reasons for the poor morale of workers in her department, she hasn't been able

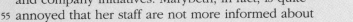

to find the source of the problem. "Besides," she
thinks to herself, "I have so much work to do. If I
80 spend all my time holding everyone's hand, how
will I ever get my work done?"

While Marybeth has spent her time with her
nose to the ground, working hard to prove herself,
Elyse has been busy building a productive team that
85 communicates well and has implemented several
innovative and successful marketing promotions.
Elyse is confident that her career is on the upswing.
And she is right; the company has just announced
Elyse's appointment as Vice-President, Marketing.
90 Marybeth, on the other hand, is beginning to feel
that her staff don't respect her and she knows they
gossip about her, talking behind her back. When
she took the position three years ago, she hoped
she could demonstrate her competence as a worker
95 and a manager. Now she wonders if she'll have this
job in six months' time.

While there are some Elyses out there in the
world of work, there are probably more Marybeths.
Many workers are determined to prove their compe-
100 tence as effective workers, managers and company
team members, yet underestimate the importance of
good communication and team-building in doing so.
Among the skills North American employers look
for in potential and promotable employees, commu-
105 nication consistently ranks in the top three in all
major surveys. But, in spite of the fact that colleges
and universities are placing greater emphasis on
developing reading, writing, and listening skills,
many of us do not excel in communicating
110 effectively with others. On the contrary, we lack the
communication skills needed to work effectively.
Perhaps we have misunderstood what good
communication means; it means much more than
speaking and writing English well. Effective commu-
115 nication is a style of behaviour that promotes and
encourages the clear expression of ideas and knowledge. It is a behaviour that can be learned and, as
illustrated in the case above, has a great impact on
our success in the workplace.

Locate the expressions below in the reading and write the
line number for each in the parentheses provided. Then
write the meaning of these expressions based on their context in the reading.

1. to set the tone ( )

_____

2. (to do something) religiously ( )

_____

3. to get off on the wrong foot ( )

_____

4. to develop (or have) a good rapport with someone ( )

_____

5. to feel (or be) left in the dark about something ( )

_____

6. number cruncher ( )

_____

7. open-door policy ( )

_____

8. to hold someone's hand (handholding) ( )

_____

9. to talk behind someone's back ( )

_____

Exercise C

1. Underline all the coordinating conjunctions of contrast
(but; yet) in the reading.

2. Double underline all the subordinate conjunctions of
contrast (although; though; even though; while;
whereas; in spite of the fact that; despite) in the reading.

3. Circle all the transition words and phrases of contrast
(however; still; nevertheless; nonetheless; on the
contrary; even so; on the other hand).

Exercise D

1. Complete the following diagram to show the similarities (the shared part of the circles) and differences
(the separated parts of the circles) between Elyse
Meyers and Marybeth Armstrong. Then write five sentences that show the similarities and five sentences that
show the differences between the two managers. Use
as many words and expressions of contrast as possible.

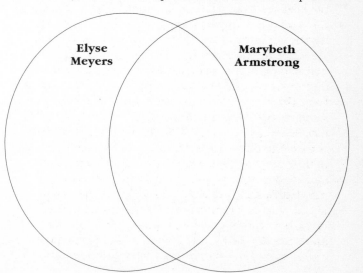

Exercise E

The connecting words and transitional expressions in some of the sentences below are incorrect. Put an [X] in the box beside the sentences with inappropriate transitional expressions or connecting words. Then rewrite the inappropriate sentences with appropriate connectors.

1. Children in the United States attend school for 180 days per year **and** students in Japan attend school 240 days per year.

2. Americans are friendly people; **on the contrary**, they don't like to be touched.

3. Monochronic people do one thing at a time; **nonetheless,** polychronic people do many things at once.

4. **Even so**, the same gesture can mean different things in different countries, the meaning of gestures can easily be learned.

5. **While** the top two cultural values of Americans are freedom and independence, the top values of Arabs are family security and family harmony.

6. People from different cultures may have dramatically different styles of communicating. **Even so**, it is possible to overcome cultural barriers to communicate effectively.

7. Latin Americans tend to build lifetime relationships, **in spite of the fact that** the British are accustomed to short-term relationships.

8. In Germany it is acceptable to talk about politics in casual conversation. In Mexico, **however**, this topic should be avoided.

9. **Although** the Japanese are sometimes hierarchical, placing great importance on age and seniority, they also value group consensus and cooperation.

10. Enrique adjusted quickly to his life in Australia. Diego, **yet**, experienced many months of frustration before he felt comfortable.

Exercise F

The sentences below express contrasts. Rewrite each sentence using different contrastive words and expressions without changing the meaning of the sentence. Pay attention to punctuation.

1. A bilingual child may speak English at school, but switch to Polish, Spanish, or Cantonese at home.

   a) yet: _____

   _____

b) although: _____

_____

c) whereas: _____

_____

2. In one study on bilingual education in New York City, researchers found that students who were taught most of their classes in English learned English well, whereas students who were taught different subjects in their primary language did not learn English well.

   a) while: _____

   _____

   b) however: _____

   _____

   c) on the other hand: _____

   _____

3. Although it is more difficult to learn a second language in adulthood, it is not impossible.

   a) even though: _____

   _____

   b) though: _____

   _____

   c) nonetheless: _____

   _____

4. Even though Sari Kristiina moved to North America in her forties without having learned any English, she managed to learn English with native-like fluency.

   a) even so: _____

   _____

   b) in spite of the fact that: _____

   _____

   c) still: _____

   _____

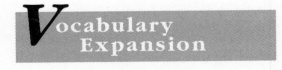

Reread the article "Want to Do Better on the Job?" on pages 59–60 in your Student Book and then complete the following exercises.

Exercise A

Write each word/phrase from the list below in the appropriate category.

blurt out	tune in (to)	(to) tune out
listen up	cut off	grasp
bite your tongue	buzz-word	

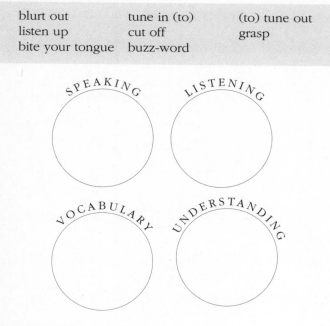

Exercise B

Replace the underlined words in each sentence with a form of the expressions from Exercise A.

1. I didn't think it wise to tell my boss his idea was terrible so I stopped myself from saying anything.

2. I can't discuss drugs with my teenager because every time I broach the subject, he doesn't listen.

3. You have three minutes to present your arguments. After three minutes, you will be stopped from talking.

4. I only asked him how things were going, when he suddenly, without thinking of the consequences, told me about this terrible secret.

5. No matter how many times the teacher explains this concept, I can't understand it.

6. "Empowerment" was the word that was fashionable in the late 1980s and early 1990s.

7. Okay, class. Pay attention! There's going to be a test.

8. He's a great listener. He's really aware of her feelings on the subject.

Paragraphs that compare and contrast

Comparison and contrast paragraphs detail the similarities and differences between people, objects, or items, such as the similarities and differences in the communication styles of men and women. Similarly, a comparison/contrast paragraph can be used to show the advantages and disadvantages of each communication style. The purpose of writing such a paragraph is to persuade or inform the reader. There are two basic ways to organize a comparison/contrast paragraph. The first is to make **point-by-point comparisons**, and the second is to totally describe one item and then the other. The latter technique is also known as the **block method**.

1. Point-by-point Comparison

In this type of writing, you address each comparative point from both perspectives before moving on to the next point. For example, if you were comparing the communication styles of men and women, you would pick two or three main comparative points, such as language and directness, and then write about each one from the male and female perspective.

EXAMPLE:

Comparative Point	Perspective
1. language	- men use strong, aggressive language - women use softer language
2. directness	- men say exactly what they are thinking - women express their views indirectly, expecting the listener to decode what they really mean

This type of organization is useful when organizing complex topics. Points are clearly made because the reader is able to see the similarities and differences immediately.

2. The Block Method

Although the same points are discussed in this method as in the point-by-point method, the information is organized in blocks. For example, in the case of comparing men's and women's communication styles, you would write all about men's communication styles and then all about women's styles. The points of comparison are presented in the same order as in the point-by-point method, but the reader must make the comparison or contrast. This method is most useful for short pieces of writing, such as paragraphs and short essays, where the reader is able to easily remember all the information provided.

EXAMPLE: **The Block Method**

Perspectives of Men (comparative point)	
1. language	- men use strong, aggressive language
2. directness	- men say exactly what they are thinking

Perspectives of Women (comparative point)	
1. language	- women use softer language
2. directness	- women express their views indirectly, expecting the listener to decode what they really mean

Exercise A

Reread the essay "Communication and Success in the Workplace" and determine which method of organization the writer used when comparing and contrasting the communication styles of Elyse and Marybeth.

Exercise B

Using the information in the chart below, write a paragraph in which you compare the attributes of monochronic cultures to those of polychronic cultures. Use the block method of organization. Then use the Comparison/Contrast Paragraph Checklist at the end of the unit to edit your work.

Monochronic Cultures	**Polychronic Cultures**
Do one thing at a time	Are committed to people
Concentrate on the job	Borrow and lend things often
Take time commitments seriously	Tend to build lifetime relationships
Are committed to the job	Do many things at once
Show respect for private property; rarely borrow or lend	Are highly distractable and subject to interruptions
Are accustomed to short-term relationships	Consider time commitments more casually

Rewrite the paragraph, this time using the "point-by-point" method of organization. Use the Comparison/Contrast Paragraph Checklist at the end of this unit to edit your work.

One Step Beyond — Create An Activity

Exercise C

Make a chart similar to the one in Exercise B, comparing two subjects of your choice. Exchange your chart with a classmate and write a comparison/contrast paragraph based on the information in your classmate's chart. Use the Comparison/Contrast Paragraph Checklist at the end of this unit to edit your work.

☑ **Comparison/Contrast Paragraph Checklist**

☐ Have I considered my audience and purpose (explain, persuade, or inform)?

☐ Have I narrowed my topic?

☐ Does my topic sentence state which items I am comparing/contrasting?

☐ Does my topic sentence indicate my main point (the purpose of my comparison)?

☐ Have I organized the paragraph either point-by-point or by block?

☐ Does my organization pattern suit the complexity of the topic?

☐ Have I chosen the most significant comparative/contrastive points to support the main point in my topic sentence?

☐ Do I use the same comparative/contrastive points and in the same sequence for each item of comparison?

☐ Have I used appropriate transitions to show similarities and differences?

☐ Have I checked my paragraph to make sure the meaning of each sentence is clear?

☐ Have I checked my paragraph to make sure that I have used precise words and the correct form of words?

☐ Have I proofread my paragraph for errors in grammar, punctuation, and spelling?

UNIT 5
The Cutting Edge

Vocabulary

(from the reading "The Science of *Star Trek*")

Exercise A

fantastic	alien	nonsensical
conceived	distorting	continuum
extinguished	survive	restored
rigorous	colleagues	series
binary	persnickety	novelty
expands	fiction	

Find the vocabulary words in the following Word Search. The words may be horizontal, vertical, or diagonal, and can be written forwards or backwards.

When you have located all the words, write down all the letters that you have not used, excluding the "X" letters. You should have 10 letters. Unscramble these letters and insert them in the blank to complete the sentence below.

The _____ in *Star Trek* often had some scientific validity.

Exercise B

In the following sentences, the writer has used the incorrect form of the vocabulary words from Exercise A. Write the correct form of the word above the incorrect form.

1. My cousin has a fantastic that she will become an astronaut.

2. Their survive was a complete miracle.

3. *Star Trek* was a very novelty show when it first appeared on the small screen.

4. The distorted of facts is necessary to keep to the half-hour time slot.

5. Fiction accounts of interplanetary travel abound.

6. They have a very colleague relationship.

R	B	R	C	O	N	C	E	I	V	E	D	X	N	X
X	I	X	E	X	T	X	X	X	X	X	O	X	O	X
X	N	G	C	S	X	X	X	X	X	T	X	X	N	X
E	A	Y	O	X	T	X	X	A	L	I	E	N	S	X
V	R	Y	N	R	S	O	X	X	X	N	X	S	E	L
I	Y	X	T	E	O	X	R	X	E	G	N	D	N	S
V	X	X	I	L	X	U	X	E	X	U	O	N	S	E
R	O	R	N	X	E	X	S	X	D	I	I	A	I	U
U	E	X	U	X	X	V	X	X	X	S	T	P	C	G
S	X	X	U	X	X	G	O	X	C	H	C	X	A	A
X	X	X	M	X	X	X	X	N	X	E	I	E	L	E
F	A	N	T	A	S	T	I	C	X	D	F	X	X	L
X	X	G	N	I	T	R	O	T	S	I	D	X	X	L
X	X	X	N	X	X	X	X	X	X	H	X	X	X	O
X	P	E	R	S	N	I	C	K	E	T	Y	X	X	C

7. From the show's conceive, Roddenberry strove for scientific accuracy.

8. The rigorous of working every day and going to school at night are evident.

9. The expanded of product marketing around the world has ensured continued sales.

10. Have you seen the restore of the original *Enterprise*?

One Step Beyond — Create An Activity

Exercise C

Create sentences that incorporate 10 of the words listed in Exercise A. Where possible, use different forms of the words and leave blanks for these words when you write out the exercise. Exchange your sentences with a classmate and complete each other's exercise.

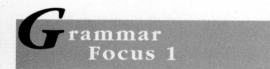

NOUN CLAUSES

Exercise A

Noun clauses often follow verbs of mental activity. (See Student Book, Appendix page 159.) Reread the article "The Science of *Star Trek*" and answer the following questions using noun clauses.

1. What surprising fact did you learn about *Star Trek*?

   _____

   _____

2. What have you learned about the scientific validity of the show?

   _____

   _____

3. What have you realized about the type of people the show appeals to?

   _____

   _____

4. What are two new things that you learned about science?

   _____

   _____

5. Is there anything that you no longer believe about the show?

   _____

   _____

6. What do you feel is the most appealing thing about the show to the author of the article, Dr. David Allen Batchelor?

   _____

   _____

Exercise B

Although *Star Trek* got off to a shaky start, it can be credited with spawning a multi-billion dollar "Trekkie" empire. Initially this fantastical science fiction show bombed in its late-night time slot. After a disastrous three seasons, it went into syndication and was placed in the after-school lineup, enabling kids to watch the series every day and resulting in the birth of "Trekkies." Trekkie-mania swept across North America as fans of the show flocked to Trekkie conventions dressed in their spacesuits and sporting Vulcan ears. The sale of Trekkie memorabilia alone is worth over $3 million a year. More than 145 books have been written about *Star Trek*. In 1979, Roddenberry, the creator of *Star Trek*, successfully took his TV show to the big screen with *Star Trek: The Motion Picture*. Its wild success led to many more feature movies. Two generations have grown up on *Star Trek* and its spin-offs. These spin-offs, such as *Star Trek: The Next Generation* and *Deep Space Nine*, continue to enjoy vast popularity. Gene Roddenberry's vision of the future turned into an extremely profitable empire that has no end in sight.

Summarize the paragraph by filling in the blanks with noun clauses.

1. The fact that _____

   didn't prevent it from spawning a multi-billion dollar

   industry.

2. Its syndicated placement in the after-school lineup

   ensured that _____ .

3. The proliferation of Trekkie conventions, books, and

   memorabilia proved that _____

   _____ .

4. The movies and spin-offs prove that _____

   _____ .

Exercise C

Restate the objects of the following sentences using a noun clause that begins with a question word.

EXAMPLE: Alicia doesn't know the **date** of the new movie's release.

Alicia doesn't know **when the new movie is being released.**

1. Lee is unaware of the **location** of the filming.

   _____

   _____

2. You will be impressed by the **number of returning stars** we have signed.

   _____

   _____

3. Do you know her **reason for watching the show**?

   _____

   _____

4. Are you aware of the **timing** of the publicity campaign kickoff?

   _____

   _____

5. I can't identify the **best actor** on the show.

   _____

   _____

Exercise D

Complete the following sentences with a noun clause in the object position. Be careful of tense changes.

1. I like to watch reruns of *Star Trek* even though I've seen them all several times. This addiction, according to my best friend, is incomprehensible. He can't understand **why** _____

   _____

2. I explained **that** _____

   _____

3. He wanted to know **what** _____

   _____

4. He also wanted to know **how long** _____

   _____

5. I couldn't remember exactly **when** _____

   _____

6. Roddenberry never knew **how**

   _____

   _____

7. Nor did he envision **how** _____

   _____

8. I wonder if my friend will ever understand **what**

   _____

   _____

Grammar Expansion

In conversation, when responding affirmatively to a yes/no question, "so" can be used in place of the "that" clause after certain verbs such as *hope, think, believe, assume, suppose, be afraid, guess, imagine, it appears,* and *it seems.*

EXAMPLE: Was the experiment a success?

I believe **so**. (so = that the experiment was a success)

A negative response can be formed by the negative verb + *so* or the verb + *not.*

EXAMPLE: Was the experiment a success?

I **don't believe so.**

I **believe not**.

Note: The verbs *be afraid, guess,* and *hope* can only be followed by *not* in a negative sentence.

Exercise E

You are being interviewed by a local newspaper reporter. Respond to the reporter's questions using a negative or positive response, and substituting "so" for the "that" clause. Add another line to explain your response.

EXAMPLE: *Reporter:* Was the original *Star Trek* initially a success?

You: I don't think so. It only achieved popularity once it was syndicated.

Note: You could respond "I think not"; however, when that construction is used with the verb "think," it produces either a very formal, condescending tone or a sarcastic one.

1. R: Would you be interested in attending a *Star Trek* convention?

   Y: _____

   _____

2. R: Are people who attend these conventions weird?

Y: _____

_____

3. R: Have you seen pictures of people attending the conventions dressed in their favourite costumes?

Y: _____

_____

4. R: Are the original shows sexist in any way?

Y: _____

_____

5. R: Will they continue to be popular for generations to come?

Y: _____

_____

6. R: Would you let your children watch a *Star Trek* movie at age eight?

Y: _____

_____

Grammar In Use

Exercise F

Underline the noun clauses in the following quotations. Then write a few sentences after each quotation, outlining your response to it. Use noun clauses or substitutes for noun clauses in your response.

That is the glory of science — that science is tentative, that it is not certain, that it is subject to change.

Isaac Asimov

_____

_____

_____

This constant striving to match newly acquired experiential knowledge with the traditions of physics is a kind of learning, or a kind of endeavour, which I did not learn in China. It encouraged me to think about what people had not found before, not just to learn what I was told to learn.

Chen Ning Yang — physicist

_____

_____

It was thought that technological advances would benefit mankind. Instead of saving work, (electrical "labour-saving") devices permit everybody to do his own work. What the 19th century had delegated to servants and housemaids, we now do for ourselves.

Marshall McLuhan

_____

_____

_____

Vocabulary 1

Exercise A

There are six errors in preposition collocations in the following passage. Circle them and correct them.

There has been a long, ongoing debate of the ability of the planet Mars to sustain life forms. Many scientists with degrees about astronomy and geology have studied grainy, distant photos attempting to unlock the

5   mysteries of the red planet.

As a result of a recent mission to Mars, the Pathfinder's "Sojourner" is transmitting photos of the planet's surface back to earth, enabling scientists to get a close-up look at the red planet for the first time.

10 The sophisticated robot has gathered samples into the surface rocks. Its analysis into the planet's surface is an attempt to determine the components. A recent examination on Mars' atmosphere indicates that it contains water and ice particles. As scientists continue

15 to receive accurate, reliable data from the robot, countless articles to their findings will be published in journals dedicated to new developments in science.

One Step Beyond — Create An Activity

Exercise B

Find an interesting newspaper article about science or technology. Rewrite the article leaving blanks for all prepositions coming after a noun. Then exchange the article with a partner who should fill in the appropriate prepositions.

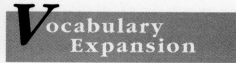

Vocabulary Expansion

Exercise C

Read the following dialogue and try to determine the meaning of the bolded idioms from the context. Then think of situations in your own life when you might use some of these idiomatic expressions and complete the chart below.

Reporter: The life of a scientist must be a very glamorous one.

Scientist: Not really. Funding is difficult to get and you are constantly **under pressure** to get results from your research. I spend many an evening poised over a microscope **burning the midnight oil**.

Reporter: Don't you have research assistants helping you?

Scientist: Sometimes, if I'm lucky. Regardless, I have to **roll up my sleeves and dig in** in order to conduct my experiments. There is a lot of labour that goes into a project before anyone even hears about its existence.

Reporter: How do you **figure out** what is really relevant in your findings?

Scientist: Most of it is from testing and retesting to check for validity. There are certain guidelines to determine whether your findings are significant or not. It's possible to have worked for months only to **find out** that your results are virtually meaningless.

Reporter: What has been the most exciting project you have worked on to date?

Scientist: That would be my last project. I had given up all hope of succeeding, and my funding was to run out within days, when **out of the blue** new information came to light which greatly influenced my results and ensured that my funding would be renewed.

Reporter: I guess you could say the new information came **just in the nick of time**.

Scientist: Absolutely.

Idioms	Meaning	Real-Life Situations
be under pressure		
burn the midnight oil		
roll up one's sleeves and dig in		
figure out		
find out		
out of the blue		
in the nick of time		

Grammar Focus 2

FUNCTIONS OF NOUN CLAUSES

Exercise A

Review the different functions of noun clauses on page 72 in the Student Book. Underline the noun clauses in the following sentences and state their grammatical function.

1. It's a good thing that governments have strict regulations about how far scientists can go.

    Function: _____

2. That aliens have visited earth is a completely ludicrous suggestion.

    Function: _____

3. The idea that we could limit human cloning to replacement parts for people is just sick.

    Function: _____

4. The theory is that we will be making regular trips to Mars in the near future.

    Function: _____

5. It seems likely that scientists will try to clone humans in the future.

    Function: _____

6. An official inquiry will look into who was responsible for the mix-up.

    Function: _____

7. Sahib was doubtful that his view of the future would be shared by others.

    Function: _____

Grammar In Use

Exercise B

Complete the following sentences by providing noun clause subjects.

EXAMPLE: _____ is a mystery to us.

> **Whether there is life on Mars** is a mystery to us.

1. _____ worries me.

2. _____ is of

    concern to everyone.

3. _____ supports

    the notion that there is life on other planets.

4. _____ demonstrates that many people are uncomfortable with gene manipulation.

5. _____ is a huge problem.

6. _____ is not universally accepted.

Exercise C

The following descriptions outline some technological developments. Record your thoughts about the developments in a sentence using the following structure: **The fact/idea/news/discovery + "that" noun clause.**

EXAMPLE: The Canadarm is a large Canadian-made robotic arm which allows astronauts aboard US space missions to do repairs.

> *The fact that an important part of the US spacecraft is Canadian shows the cooperation between the two countries.*

1. The Internet initially had limited use, with the military and scholars being the main users. Since it has been made accessible to the public, it has enabled millions to have information at their fingertips. Regulating the new electronic medium remains a challenge for police who attempt to track down cyberspace criminals.

    _____

    _____

2. The original computer filled an entire room. Thirty-five years later this monster had been reduced in size to a machine able to sit on a desktop. Only ten years after that, the computer was reduced to the size of a laptop. The size, convenience, and affordability of computers have made them an integral part of our daily lives. If the current trend continues, all homes will have a computer in the near future.

    _____

    _____

3. Cars that burn fossil fuels continue to pollute our air. Scientists have been experimenting unsuccessfully with electric cars. As yet, they have not found a way to make them cheap and powerful. Now they are looking at hydrogen fuel cells. These fuel cells work by combining hydrogen and oxygen. The hydrogen can be obtained from water, natural gas, or municipal waste, using electricity or heat. This type of fuel production would have no impact on the environment. The challenge is to make the engines much cheaper than the several thousands of dollars they currently

cost. Perhaps within the decade we will be driving environmentally-friendly cars.

_____

_____

4. Studies of DNA have allowed scientists to identify the genes responsible for deadly diseases, and in some cases repair these genes. In the near future, researchers hope to be able to recode defective genes in order to make them start working correctly. This would allow for the reversal of terminal diseases like cancer.

_____

_____

5. Virtual reality is a powerful technology. It is currently being used to train pilots using simulated flights that are incredibly realistic. Doctors have been able to use 3-D images from CAT-scans to recreate a person's insides, thus locating problems faster and easier than with traditional X-rays. Helmets and goggles are being developed that will enable the wearer to enter a virtual world and take "totally virtual" vacations.

_____

_____

Exercise D

Complete the following sentences using noun clauses as objects of the prepositions.

EXAMPLE: Everyone has heard **about**...

> Everyone has heard about **what scientists have achieved in their cloning experiments**.

1. I am especially interested **in** _____

_____

2. Do you honestly approve **of** _____

_____

3. The studies focus **on** _____

_____

4. In the future they will look **at** _____

_____

5. People cannot rely **on** _____

_____

6. Do you agree **with** _____

_____

Exercise E — Editing

Scientists recently announced that they had successfully cloned a sheep. Many people were concerned about the possible implications of this success. The following sentences discuss this topic. Note that the sentences

contain errors in their use of noun clauses. Underline these errors and write the correct form above the error.

1. People asked why wanted the scientists to do this type of experiment.

2. The scientists indicated them that they hoped to gain insights into cell growth.

3. The people asked if they had considered the possible negative implications to the scientists.

4. According to the scientists, it was important that be done this type of research despite the possible negative implications.

5. The people told the scientists that would like to see genetic manipulation stopped immediately.

6. What would that do is prevent scientists from creating human clones.

7. Working together, the people and scientists discussed how could they continue research in a limited way.

Vocabulary 2

Exercise A

Match the following roots to appropriate word parts to build words. Several word parts may fit each root. Use a separate sheet of paper.

auto	graph	patho
dyn	bio	geo
astro	cyclo	

litho	chemistry	gen
psy	para	asty
nomy	tele	naut
logical	mobile	politics
degradable	cracy	rhythm
logist	crat	mat
logy	amo	amic
centric	meter	mation
physics	amism	photo
metry	ne	

EXAMPLE: *bio* + degradable = biodegradable
          tele + *graph* = telegraph

One Step Beyond — Create an Activity

Exercise B

Select 10 words from the list you created in Exercise A that you are unfamiliar with. Look up their meanings in the dictionary. Write definitions for them in your own words. Exchange these definitions with a partner and try to identify which words are being defined.

Writing

The Expository Paragraph

The expository paragraph explains or analyzes an idea. The writer uses specific details and examples to support his/her value judgement or opinion about the topic. An anecdote or illustration can also be used to support the topic sentence. Expository writing is very common in scientific and medical fields.

An effective expository paragraph:

1. ...explains or analyzes an idea.
2. ...indicates the attitude of the writer towards the subject.
3. ...is arranged in a logical order (generally order of importance, order of familiarity, or time).
4. ...includes only those aspects and details that support the controlling idea in the topic sentence.
5. ...provides examples that accurately illustrate main points.
6. ...sufficiently explains examples to show how they support the controlling idea in the topic sentence.
7. ...uses transitional expressions *(another example, to illustrate, for instance, to begin with, furthermore, in addition)* to link the examples.

Exercise A

Write topic sentences for the following outlines.

Outline 1

1. At a large car manufacturing plant, automation has eliminated the need for thousands of workers.

2. At the utility companies, work staff was reduced with the introduction of computer-controlled processes.

3. Small offices have been able to reduce staff by increasing their use of office automation.

Outline 2

1. Elizabeth Taylor has always supported AIDS research.

2. Jennifer Aniston has lent her support to AIDS-fundraising.

3. Heather Tomm helps out regularly at AIDS hospices.

Exercise B

Circle the controlling idea in the following topic sentences. Write examples of an anecdote or illustration to support each sentence.

1. Advances in technology have enabled us to explore areas where no human has visited.

   _____

   _____

   _____

2. Gene manipulation has gone too far.

   _____

   _____

   _____

3. *Star Trek* has had many successful spin-offs.

   _____

   _____

   _____

Exercise C

In the following paragraph, identify the following:

1. the topic sentence
2. the controlling idea
3. the way the examples are sequenced (by importance, time, familiarity, for example).
4. the examples that support the controlling idea (please underline)

Cloning has been a popular subject for Hollywood movies. The earliest attempts at cloning could be seen in the *Frankenstein* movies. Scientists attempted to create their own being by replicating body parts. In 1978, Hollywood unleashed the classic cloning movie called *The Boys From Brazil,* in which a demented Dr. Josef Mengele created a number of blue-eyed, black-haired boys from the skin and blood of Adolf Hitler in a diabolical attempt to resurrect The Third Reich with these Hitler clones. A more recent human-cloning blockbuster had more benign intentions for its clones. A fun-loving husband finds the demands on his time to be too much. The movie, entitled *Multiplicity,* has Michael Keaton as an overworked construction foreman who replicates himself with the help of a local geneticist. Each clone has a distinct personality and the high jinks they get up to provide a good laugh. Now with all the debate that the real-life cloning of "Dolly" the sheep has stirred, Hollywood is sure to keep pumping out cloning movies.

Editing

Exercise D

The following outlines contain sentences with structural problems. In addition, there are flaws in the sequencing of the examples. Rewrite the outlines, rearranging the supporting examples so that they follow a logical sequence, and then correct the sentences with structural problems.

Outline 1

Topic Sentence: Downsizing in companies as a result in technological advances has had a tremendous personal impact about workers.

Example: It's been documented about that men who lose their jobs sometimes have serious problems with their families.

Example: It's the idea that they no longer useful are that leads some men into personal depression.

Example: It is a fact that many men have been in their late fifties who laid off have been unable to rejoin the workforce and consequently are losing everything they had ever.

Outline 2

Topic Sentence: Advances in technological have created increasingly destructive weapons of war.

Example: The fact about that guns enabled soldiers to kill at greatly distances increased the bloodshed conflicts incredibly.

Example: That soldiers when could only kill when at arm's length from each other had limited casualties to some extent.

Example: The fact that nuclear bombs annihilate can instantly everything within a wide radius of landing has brought unlimited killing capacity from war.

Exercise E

Choose one of the outlines and write a paragraph. You will have to further clarify the examples and provide transitions.

Exercise F

Write an expository paragraph about one of the following topics. Start with an outline. Use the Expository Paragraph Checklist at the end of the unit to edit your work.

1. Human cloning
2. Impact of science fiction
3. Future travel
4. Technological developments

☑ **Expository Paragraph Checklist**

☐ Have I considered my audience and purpose?

☐ Have I narrowed my topic?

☐ Does my topic sentence indicate what will be explained and what my attitude or opinion towards it is? (controlling idea)

☐ Have I organized my paragraph logically with my examples presented in their order of importance, order of familiarity, or time order?

☐ Have I ensured that all the examples are sufficiently explained and that the link to the controlling idea is clear?

☐ Have I used transitional expressions adequately and appropriately?

☐ Have I checked my paragraph to make sure the meaning of each sentence is clear?

☐ Have I checked my paragraph to make sure that I have used precise words and the correct form of words?

☐ Have I proofread my paragraph for errors in grammar, punctuation, and spelling?

UNIT 6
It Stands To Reason

Here's a puzzle. How many uses can you find for this ordinary building brick?

Exercise A

Seven words are used in an inappropriate grammatical form in the reading below. Find the words and replace them with an appropriate form.

Logic is a form of thinking that is valued in many cultures. The ability to reasonable is developed from very early on. As early as kindergarten, children learn to draw conclude from facts, to categorize information
5 into logical groupings, and to understand analog. The classic math problems learned in grade school, that we thought tested the ability to do sums, were really designed to develop the ability to reason. "If Johnny buys half as many eggs as his brother, and his brother
10 buys six dozen, how many eggs does Johnny buy?" This might seem like a simple math problem, but it is the first step in learning how to interpret facts to draw logical conclusions.

Grouping information into logical categories is not
15 only useful in developing skills of deduce, but also in learning how to write in English. We love categories. Anyone who learns how to write an English essay will

learn how to categorize information in both the planning and writing of the essay. As children, we were
20 drilled in exercises asking us: "Which item doesn't fit?" Look at the picture of the raincoat, the umbrella, the rain boots, and the sandals — which one doesn't fit?

We were learning how to group items, ideas, and thoughts. These activities were really precursors to writ-
25 ing. Activities in which we had to look for similarities, and then relate them to other similarities, were abundant. In the beginning, it was "what two items are alike?", but we quickly moved to "eye is to eyelid as window is to _____". These were not designed just
30 as fun word games; they developed our ability to understand relationships, a thinking skill that becomes critical in solving problems in our daily lives.

Of course, as we got older we were exposed to problems that required more creative solutions. "The
35 city council is trying to battle youth crime in a neighbourhood known for its high unemployment and drug problem. What can the community do?" Finding

solutions to these types of problems requires critical thinking skills and ingenious. Developing ration

40 thought is deemed essential in North American culture as it is in much of the world. Ignore may be bliss, but it is not very useful in our advanced social structure. And if we are to realize our full potential as thinking human beings, we must continue to exercise our minds

45 through critical thought as we exercise our bodies through physical activities: but that's an analogy that just stands to reason.

Exercise B

Find definitions for the following words and then fill in the blanks with forms of the words.

argument	opinion	riddle
puzzle	wisdom	knowledge
spatial	physical	

1. The _____ layout of the bank's new lobby was designed according to the needs of customers.

2. The newly-hired MBA* graduate was very _____ about her subject specialty, but she lacked the interpersonal skills to do the job well.

3. We will never solve the world's environmental problems until we address world hunger and poverty. What is your _____ ?

4. No matter how much you know, _____ only comes with experience.

5. Can you solve this _____ ? I am black and white and "red" all over. What am I?

6. Cartographers must have well-developed _____ intelligence to design maps.

7. Because of his weak _____ , the speaker was unable to convince his audience that child labour is a serious problem.

8. The detective was _____ by the conflicting evidence in the murder case.

* MBA (Masters of Business Administration): in North America, an advanced degree in business.

"IF" STATEMENTS (CONDITIONALS)

Exercise A

Match the sentence parts from Column A to those in Column B.

Column A	Column B
1. If the school year were extended,	a. teachers wouldn't have needed to spend so much time reviewing last year's material
2. If more emphasis were placed on learning how to learn,	b. students are more likely to be successful later in life
3. If you really want to learn a second language,	c. students will not forget what they've learned so easily
4. If the school year had been extended,	d. immerse yourself in it
5. If more emphasis had been placed on learning how to learn,	e. students would find continuous learning more agreeable
6. If more emphasis is placed on learning how to learn,	f. you would study it in school
7. If you really wanted to learn a second language,	g. students would not necessarily learn more
8. If the school year is extended,	h. the employees would have found it easier to adapt to the technological changes in the workplace

Exercise B

Some of the following sentences are correct, others are incorrect. Mark whether the sentence is correct (C) or incorrect (I). Then correct the incorrect sentences.

1. I would have done better in school if my parents encouraged me more.
2. You are less likely to achieve your full potential if you do not lead a healthy lifestyle.
3. If the parents provided a more stimulating environment for the infant, his intellect would have developed more.
4. Students learn English better if they will read a variety of materials.
5. You can learn almost anything if you are motivated.
6. If a child learns to love learning, half the battle would be won.
7. If she believed that learning increases your enjoyment of life, she would make more of an effort to learn.

Exercise C

Read the facts presented in the following sentences. Then create new sentences that suggest how the situation could be changed.

EXAMPLE: *Fact:* Jeremy didn't study for the test so he didn't do well.

Response: If Jeremy had studied for the test, he would have done better.

EXAMPLE: *Fact:* The student registered at this college but is not sure whether he has a student identification (ID) number.

Response: If the student *registered* at this college, (then) the student *has* a student identification number.

EXAMPLE: *Fact:* I don't know the answer; that's why I didn't tell you.

Response: If I *knew* the answer, I *would have told* you then.

EXAMPLE: *Fact:* You didn't finish high school. Your chances of finding a job now are not good.

Response: If you *had finished* high school, you *would have* a better chance of finding a job now.

Note: The tense of the verb in the result clause can vary according to the situation.

1. Randa values education so she studies hard.

_____

_____

2. As a young man, Peter was interested in science so he became an engineer.

_____

_____

3. Margaret is a teacher so she knows what will be expected of her children when they get to high school.

_____

_____

4. Cosmo never liked to write so he didn't write very often.

_____

_____

5. Tina takes her young daughter Chloë to the library every week so Chloë feels very comfortable there.

_____

_____

6. Chris began piano lessons at the age of four so now at the age of six he already plays quite well.

_____

_____

7. Nicholas is very interested in science so his mother sent him to science camp in the summer.

_____

_____

8. Young Martin spends a lot of time with his Spanish-speaking grandparents so he speaks Spanish as well as English.

_____

_____

Grammar In Use
Exercise D

Education reform is popular in many countries of the world. What changes could be made to the education system in your country of origin, and what consequences would these changes have? Write ten sentences that state your point of view.

EXAMPLE: If students were given more homework in my country, they would learn better study habits.

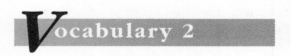

Vocabulary 2

Phrasal Verbs
Exercise A

Fill in the blanks with a form of the appropriate phrasal verb.

focus on
figure out
account for

work towards
bring about
find out

Memorandum

To: Monica Sparrow
From: Robert Dale
Date: October 1, 2003

Re: Production Meeting

In Tuesday's initial production meeting, I would like to
(1) _____ the following agenda items:

1. Scope of the Advanced English Course program
2. Skeletal outline of program contents
3. Project workback schedule

Although we have already discussed the scope of this
project with the authors in general terms, I would like to
clarify our objectives at this meeting. We will have to
(2) _____ what the essential content should
be, so please think about this before the meeting. Also,
(3) _____ what the authors plan to include in the
program before the meeting. This will not only facilitate our
discussions, but ensure that we're (4) _____
a common goal.

    You mentioned that you anticipate expenditures beyond
those (5) _____ in the original project budget.
You will need to present some good arguments if you want to
(6) _____ a change in the budget. Prepare a
memo, addressed to me, outlining what additional expenses you
anticipate. Explain why these expenses are necessary and what
the resulting benefits will be.

    Monica, I look forward to working with you on this project
and I'm certain we will once again produce an excellent product.

Exercise B

When a verb combines with an adverb or a preposition to
create a new meaning, it is called a phrasal verb. List as
many meanings as possible for the individual verbs listed
below, and then write definitions for the phrasal verbs.

1. to focus:

_____

to focus on:

_____

2. to figure:

_____

to figure out:

_____

3. to account:

_____

to account for:

_____

4. to work:

_____

to work towards:

_____

5. to bring:

_____

to bring about:

_____

6. to find:

_____

to find out:

_____

One Step Beyond — Create An Activity

Exercise C

Write a sentence using each individual verb and each phrasal verb in Exercise B. Rewrite the sentences leaving out the target phrasal verb or individual verbs. Exchange your work with a classmate and complete the activity you receive.

MODALS

Exercise A

The president has been murdered. He was stabbed 20 times. The bar line below shows how probable each fact is. Write sentences of deduction for each fact, using modals of probability.

Yes 100%

a. 95% yes — the victim screamed

b. 75% yes — the cook killed him

c. 50% yes/no — the maid saw the murderer

d. 75% no — the wife killed him (she claims to have an alibi)

No 100% **e.** 100% no — the president committed suicide

"IF" STATEMENTS WITH MODALS

Conditional sentences can also be expressed with modals. In conditional sentences, modals are used in the same way as in other sentences. The rules about tenses in conditional sentences still apply.

EXAMPLES: _(possible condition / unspecified time)_ ⟹ _(deduced result / unspecified time)_

If Lisa has a high IQ score, she _must_ be very intelligent.

(real past condition) ⟹ _(deduced past result)_

If no one _could_ understand the explanation, it _must_ have been too complicated.

Exercise B

Add words to create sentences that show a condition/result relationship. You may have to change the order of phrases.

1. study hard / have to / do well on test

_____

_____

2. know one foreign language / should / easier to learn another

_____

_____

3. write the summary / not read the book / be able to

_____

_____

4. suspect / can't / alibi / committed murder

_____

_____

5. know something about the American Civil Rights Movement / might / understand context of Martin Luther King's speech

_____

_____

Exercise C

Read the following excerpt on problem-solving from a college-level psychology text and then answer the questions that follow on a separate sheet.

BECOMING BETTER AT PROBLEM-SOLVING

The first step in successfully solving a problem is to interpret or represent the problem correctly. You can then experiment with a number of solution strategies, shifting your perspective on the problem from one angle to another. Let's look more closely at how some of these strategies work.

Tactic of elimination

If in solving a given problem you are more sure of what you do not want than of what you do want, the **tactic of elimination** can be very helpful. The best approach is first to create a list of all the possible solutions you can think of. Then discard all the solutions that take you where you definitely do not want to go. That leaves a smaller number of potential solutions for you to examine much more closely. This strategy will only work if your list of possible solutions contains at least one good solution to the problem. Otherwise you'll end up eliminating all the possible solutions on your list, and you'll have to start all over again from scratch! Also, you have to be careful not to scrap a solution that *seems* on the surface to lead to an undesirable outcome, but on closer examination, might turn out to be an excellent solution to the problem.

Visualizing

Other useful tactics include **visualizing**, diagramming, and charting various courses of action. By drawing a diagram of a problem, or even constructing a simple model of it, you may find it easier to grasp the principle of the problem and to avoid irrelevant or distracting details. Some chess masters, for example, can visualize chess games in their heads; as a result, they are able to play as many as 50 simultaneous games blindfolded!

Creative problem-solving

Many problems, of course, do not lend themselves to straightforward solutions but rely more on flexible and original thinking. For example, how many unusual uses can you think of for an ordinary object like a brick? It's easy to imagine a few good uses for a brick but quite another task to come up with 50 or 60 distinct uses.

Psychologists sometimes refer to this type of thinking as **divergent thinking**, as opposed to **convergent thinking**. A problem requiring convergent thinking has only one or a very few solutions — like a math problem. Convergent thinking is required when a problem has a known solution. By contrast, problems that have no single correct solution and that require a flexible, inventive approach, call for divergent thinking.

Because creative problem-solving requires thinking up new and original ideas, the process is not always aided by planning or the deliberate use of problem-solving strategies. Solutions to many problems rely on insight, a seemingly arbitrary flash "out of the blue" that reveals the solution to a problem. Therefore, if you simply cannot arrive at a solution to a problem after careful preparation and step-by-step efforts at problem-solving, it might be wise to stop thinking about the problem for a while and return to it later, approaching it from a new angle. Sometimes you get so enmeshed in the details of a problem that you lose sight of an obvious solution. Taking a rest from the problem may allow a fresh approach to surface.

It is also important to develop a questioning attitude toward problems. Ask yourself, "What is the real problem here? Can the problem be interpreted in other ways?" By *redefining* the problem, you may find that you have opened up new avenues to creative solutions. And try to maintain an uncritical attitude toward potential solutions: Don't reject a prospective solution because at first glance it doesn't seem to fit that problem. On closer examination, the solution may turn out to be highly effective, or it may bring to mind similar solutions that would work. This is the rationale behind the technique called **brainstorming** — when solving a problem, produce lots of ideas without evaluating them prematurely. Only after lots of ideas have been collected should you review and evaluate them.

Finally, people may become more creative when they interact with creative peers and teachers who serve as role models. Although some creative people work well in isolation, many others find it stimulating to collaborate with other creative people.

1. What should you do as a first step if you are trying to solve a problem?

2. The reading states that the "tactic of elimination" strategy will only work if one condition is met. What is the condition?

3. If the "tactic of elimination" strategy is not suitable for solving a problem, what other strategies can you use?

4. What does the reading suggest you should do if you cannot find a solution to a problem after careful preparation and step-by-step efforts?

5. What may happen if you reject a prospective solution at first glance?

Exercise D

What conclusions or expectations are logical based on the following facts? Be careful. Some facts lead to different degrees of certainty; let the meaning guide you.

EXAMPLE: a) All brothers are male.
b) I have a brother.

If all brothers are male, and I have a brother, my brother must be male.

1. a) All carnivores eat meat.
   b) My pet is a carnivore.

   _____

   _____

2. a) Polar bears are white.
   b) This bear lives at the North Pole.

   _____

   _____

3. a) Henry lost his dog, which answers to the name Fado.
   b) Jeannie found a dog, which answers to the name Fado.

   _____

   _____

4. a) Martin's grandparents speak only Spanish.
   b) Martin spends a lot of time with his grandparents.

   _____

   _____

5. a) I have no brothers or sisters.
   b) This man is my father's son.

   _____

   _____

6. a) The mystery word has three letters and is a synonym for "happy."
   b) The mystery word does not contain the letter "j."

   _____

   _____

7. a) The teacher received an essay from an unidentified student about the American Civil Rights Movement.
   b) Only two students in the class wrote an essay on this topic.
   c) John wrote an essay on the great explosion at Halifax Harbour in 1917.
   d) Each student wrote only one essay.

   _____

   _____

8. a) Anita's mother is Francophone.
   b) Anita lives in Edmonton.
   c) Anita is bilingual.

   _____

   _____

One Step Beyond — Create An Activity
Exercise E

Create an activity like the one in Exercise D. Write eight sets of facts and exchange your facts with a classmate. Write *if/then* statements to draw logical conclusions from your classmate's facts.

Vocabulary Expansion

Expressing Cause and Effect
Exercise A

As you read this paragraph about the sources of stress, underline at least five different words or phrases that signal cause or effect.

The first step in learning to manage stress is to understand its causes. It is important to understand that stress has two defining characteristics: it is a state of tension or a feeling of threat and it requires
5 us to change or adapt. The most common source of stress is change. People prefer continuity and predictability in their lives. But change by itself isn't necessarily stressful. Consider the example of driving on a road and coming to a red light. We
10 have to change our behaviour and stop. Stopping at the red light, however, does not necessarily lead to stress. If, on the other hand, we are late for an appointment, having to stop at the red light may indeed result in stress. Stress may also result from
15 pressure. When we feel forced to speed up, intensify, or achieve a higher standard of performance, we experience pressure. Sometimes pressure is internally imposed, as in the case of personal standards of excellence. Other times it results from
20 external sources, such as the media or our peers; many people feel pressured by the need to conform to the social standards of beauty modelled on television and in magazines. A third source of stress is frustration. This is the feeling we experience when
25 we are prevented from reaching a goal because something or someone stands in our way. The worker who is by-passed for a promotion because of discriminatory practices experiences frustration. Once we understand the causes of stress, we can
30 begin to work on managing and possibly reducing it.

Words that signal cause	Words that signal effect
_____	_____
_____	_____
_____	_____
_____	_____
_____	_____
_____	_____

Add other words or phrases you know that can signal cause or effect. Use a thesaurus to help you.

Exercise B

Write sentences to express the following cause and effect relationships. Use the words and phrases you identified in Exercise A.

1. prolong life/fear death

_____

_____

2. high self-esteem/parental praise and feeling secure

_____

_____

3. smoking/cancer

_____

_____

4. infant stimulation/increase intelligence

_____

_____

5. ability to reason/exercising the mind

_____

_____

6. academic performance/nutrition and sleep

_____

_____

7. lack of exercise/poor health

_____

_____

8. criminal activity/high unemployment

_____

_____

9. relationships suffer/poor communication

_____

_____

10. explosion/gas leak

_____

_____

Writing

Cause and Effect Paragraphs

It is impossible to go through a single day in our lives without either consciously or subconsciously analyzing the causes and effects of our actions, and those of everything around us.

In the Cause and Effect paragraph, a writer seeks to understand a topic by analyzing it. When causes are analyzed, the writer attempts to understand *why* a certain event occurred. When effects are analyzed, the writer considers the *results* of a certain event. Based on the findings, the reader may also be able to predict results or effects given similar circumstances. Because of the shortness of a paragraph, the writer would normally address either the cause or the effect, but not both. The paragraph is generally organized according to familiarity or interest when the causes or effects are of equal significance. If one cause or effect is obviously more important than some of the others, the factors should be presented from most important to least important.

This type of writing is very common amongst professionals dealing with individuals, such as doctors, nurses, teachers, supervisors, psychologists, etc.

Cause and Effect paragraphs can be evaluative, where the writer indicates his or her own opinions about the cause or effect. This type of writing forces the writer to judge the information and form an opinion. The paragraph can also be informative, where the writer merely presents the facts, trying to keep the paragraph as objective as possible.

An effective Cause and Effect paragraph:

1. ...analyzes either the causes or the results of a particular event.

2. ...is arranged in a logical order (generally order of importance, order of familiarity, or time).

3. ...has a topic sentence that briefly states the causes or effects to be examined (if it is an informative paragraph), or has a controlling idea that states the writer's feelings towards the event (if it is an evaluative paragraph).

4. ...includes sufficient detail to explain the cause or effect of a particular event.

5. ...uses transitional expressions to link the causes or effects.

Exercise A

Work individually or in teams. List at least five possible **causes** for each of the following topics.

1. high unemployment
2. high crime
3. poverty

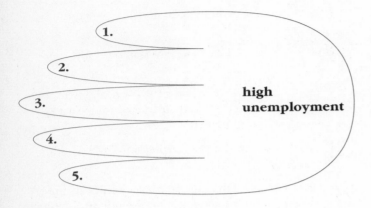

Now list at least five possible **results** for each of the following topics.

1. constant criticism
2. slackening of academic standards
3. racial prejudice

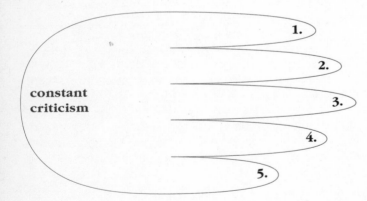

Exercise B

In order to convince the reader that the opinion or idea you expressed in a topic sentence is valid (true), you must support your ideas. You can support an idea with examples, anecdotes, statistics, definitions, or reasoning. You will have to choose what works best.

For each of the following topics, agree with one of the opinions and write three ideas that support your position.

1. The effects of parental expectations on children...
   a) Parents must continuously set high expectations for their children if the children are to achieve success.
   b) When parents continuously set high expectations for their children, they send their children a message that their worth is measured by their achievements rather than by the type of people they are.

   _____

   _____

2. Many young children today are having difficulty learning to spell...
   a) There is no proven correlation between the amount of television a young child watches and the difficulty he or she has learning to spell.
   b) Many young children today are having difficulty learning to spell because of poor reading habits.

   _____

   _____

3. The results of encouraging competition in children...
   a) Encouraging children to be competitive in sports, in academics, and in their personal relationships discourages them from sharing and cooperating with others and sets them up for failure in a work force that values teamwork.
   b) Encouraging children to be competitive in sports, in academics, and in their personal relationships encourages self-discipline and goal-setting and prepares them for the world of work.

   _____

   _____

Exercise C — Editing

Edit the following paragraph for errors in grammar and punctuation.

If I teach my children only one skill, it would be to learn how to learn. In our fast-changing technological society, if one can't learn new skills quickly and adapt to new ideas, one was lost. Gone are the days when rote learning led the way to knowledge and success. As little as 50 years ago, if you are knowledgeable you are admired. If you had a college or university degree, you were guaranteed a good job. If knowledge will be all you can offer an employer today, you're not worth hiring; today's knowledge is obsolete tomorrow. However, if you had known where and how to access knowledge you have a transferable skill that will never be obsolete. If you can understood how you, as an individual, learn best and can acquire the skills for learning, your road will have been paved with opportunity. If, on the other hand, you focus only on what you are learning, without ever understanding the process, each new learning experience may have lead to frustration and possibly failure.

Exercise D

Complete these writing activities. Use the Cause and Effect Paragraph Checklist at the end of this unit to edit your work.

1. Design a brochure for a private English-language school. Include a paragraph that explains the benefits of learning English as a second language.

2. Write a speech for students about to enter high school. Discuss the causes of failing to achieve academic success in high school and the importance of becoming a successful learner.

3. Write a sales letter soliciting business for a new fitness club and health centre. Include a paragraph about the benefits of a healthy lifestyle.

✓ Cause and Effect Paragraph Checklist

- [ ] Have I considered my audience and purpose?
- [ ] Have I narrowed my topic?
- [ ] Does my topic sentence indicate if I will be discussing causes or effects?
- [ ] Have I supported my opinion if my paragraph is evaluative (opinion)?
- [ ] Have I provided enough information if my paragraph is informative (fact)?
- [ ] Have I organized my paragraph logically with my examples presented in their order of familiarity, interest, or importance?
- [ ] Have I used transitional expressions adequately and appropriately?
- [ ] Have I ensured that all the causes or effects are sufficiently explained and that the link to the topic sentence is clear?
- [ ] Have I checked my paragraph to make sure the meaning of each sentence is clear?
- [ ] Have I checked my paragraph to make sure that I have used precise words and the correct form of words?
- [ ] Have I proofread my paragraph for errors in grammar, punctuation, and spelling?

UNIT 7
All the Rage

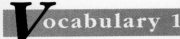

Exercise A

Search for the words from the fill-in-the-blanks exercise below and circle them in the word grid provided. The words may be written horizontally, vertically, or diagonally, and can be written forwards or backwards. One example has been done for you.

r	t	i	v	f	k	a	p	k	l	m
t	r	r	d	e	m	l	o	d	i	l
g	i	m	m	i	c	k	s	e	b	h
n	v	o	a	i	t	o	c	p	t	c
h	i	p	n	i	n	r	i	y	c	g
m	a	n	i	a	e	a	k	h	d	i
e	l	a	c	n	r	o	m	l	a	m
r	n	o	e	r	t	r	e	n	d	s

1. Some rock stars in the 1970s used ___gimmicks___ such as smashing their guitars and setting the stage on fire to attract attention and create excitement.

2. Hollywood blockbuster films are often _____ with massive advertising and merchandising to persuade the public to see them.

3. It's amazing how many people buy trashy entertainment magazines to quench their thirst for show business _____ .

4. Frank Sinatra, Hollywood music and film _____ of the 1940s, was worshipped by millions of adoring fans.

5. The current North American _____ for the paranormal explains the success of shows like *The X-Files*.

6. North American fashion _____ over the last 100 years have ranged from the long, elegant, and well-fitted gowns of the 1930s and 1940s, to the funky look of the 1960s.

Exercise B

For each of the nouns in the left column, write another grammatical form of the word as indicated in parentheses. Then write a sentence for each of your words on a separate sheet of paper.

idol   (verb)   _____

trivia   (adjective) _____

craze   (adjective) _____

gimmick   (adjective) _____

trend   (adjective) _____

mania   (adjective) _____

hype   (verb)   _____

One Step Beyond — Create An Activity
Exercise C

Design a crossword puzzle for your classmates using eight words from this unit. Incorporate each word in a sentence and leave a blank for the missing word.

EXAMPLE: **Across: 1.** John Lennon of "The Beatles" was more than a rock star; with his messages of peace, he was an _____ for the youth of his generation. (Answer: icon)

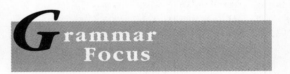

TO + BASE VERBALS
Exercise A

Read the text below about some popular games played in North America and then answer the questions.

Parlour Games
Parlour is an old word and was the name given to a room in a private house for sitting in, relaxing, or entertaining visitors. A parlour game is a game played in the home, usually with words or actions. Playing parlour
5 games was very popular in North America before television and radio. Even today, many North Americans enjoy playing these games at parties. Some parlour games are no more than tricks, but others challenge our intellect and wit and appeal to keen competitors as

10 much as do the best card and board games. Most
parlour games require no special equipment beyond
pencils and paper, and sometimes not even that.

Charades

Played in several different forms, and variously known
as "The Game," Quotations, and Charades, this is a
15 team game — and the more people on the team the
better.

First the teams are formed. It is best if two captains
are appointed, and they leave the room to choose up
sides. Then the teams separate. Each team decides, and
20 writes on a slip of paper, a quotation, name, or phrase
for each member of the other team. (An alternative is to
assign phrases in different categories — for example, a
movie title, an actor, or a popular song title.) The player
to whom that quotation, name, or phrase is assigned
25 must act it out in such a way that his or her teammates
will be able to guess it.

The teams now reassemble. One by one, the players
take their turns, with the teams alternating. While each
team performs, the opposing team sits back and
30 watches. While the player acts out his or her stint,
teammates try to guess what he or she is driving at.

The rules are:
- Players who are doing the acting may utter no
  sound. They may point to people in the room to put
35 over an idea, but may not use any "props" — furniture, fixtures, or any other inanimate (or animate!)
  object.
- Players may use gestures, gesticulations, and other
  forms of acting as much as they please, except that
40 they may not form letters with their hands or with
  their mouths to spell out a word.
- The players' teammates may talk as much as they
  please, and ask whatever questions they please, and
  the player may use appropriate gestures to tell them
45 whether they are right or wrong, and whether they
  are getting close or are not on the right track.

For example, suppose a player must act out
Baltimore, (a city in the United States). She chooses
to start by tossing imaginary balls into the air, as
50 though she were a juggler. Her teammates guess,
rapidly, "Juggler...circus...parade..." etc., and each
time she shakes her head "No." She stops and
describes a ball with her hands, then confirms the
fact that they are right by any appropriate gesture.
55 Similarly she will act out "tea" then "more," then
signal to her teammates to say all three in order,
getting "Ball-tea-more."
- Time is kept on each player, and a record made of
  how many seconds or minutes it took for his or her
60 teammates to guess the phrase. The team which
  uses the least time to guess all its assignments is the
  winner. Usually a time limit, such as five minutes, is
  placed on each player; but good players seldom
  exceed two minutes for even a difficult assignment.

Glossary

(18-19) *choose up sides* — select who will play on each
team
(30) *stint* — a task that is completed in a specific time
(34-35) *put over an idea* — make others understand
(36) *inanimate* — not alive
(38) *gesticulations* — movement of the hands or arms
to emphasize a word
(46) *getting close* — thinking in the right way

Questions

1. What is the object of the game?

   The object of the game is _____

   _____ .

2. According to the instructions, why do the team
   captains leave the room?

   The team captains leave the room _____

   _____ .

3. What should a player's teammates do while he or she
   is acting out a phrase?

   Teammates should try _____

   _____ .

4. What can't players use to get their ideas across?

   Players can't use _____ .

5. Why would players point to people in the room as
   they are acting out their assignments?

   Players might point to people in the room _____

   _____ .

6. For what purpose do players use gestures in this game?

   In this game, players use gestures _____

   _____ .

Exercise B

Read the text below about another popular game and then
answer the questions.

Categories

Any number may play this game, each for himself or
herself. Each player rules off a 6 x 6 diagram such as
the one illustrated below, making the spaces large
4 enough to write words in them.

5 Now categories are selected: usually there are five of them. At the start, such obvious ones as cities, animals, famous people, etc., are chosen. New categories become increasingly hard to find, but there is no reason not to repeat the old ones if new key words are
10 taken. The key word is any five-letter word in which no letter is repeated and in which there are none of the difficult letters such a Q, Z, X, (e.g., CREAM in the chart below). The object of the game is to write in each space a word fitting the category and beginning with
15 the letter of the key word at the head of that column.

	C	R	E	A	M
Major World Cities	Cali	Rome	Exeter	Ankara	Montreal
Occupations	Computer Programmer	Radio Announcer	Engineer	Architect	Musician
Languages	Croatian	Russian	English	Arabic	Mandarin
Great People	Churchill, Winston	Rousseau, Jean Jacques	Einstein, Albert	Aristotle	Mandela, Nelson
Animals	Cat	Raccoon	Elephant	Ant	Monkey

A time limit is set: 20 minutes is a convenient one. A timekeeper announces the end of the time limit, and everyone stops writing. Then the spaces are taken up one by one, each player announcing the word, if any,
20 he or she has for that space. For each space, a player scores one point for every other player who does not have the same word. The player with the greatest number of points is the winner.

Questions

1. What is the object of the game?

   The object of the game is _____

   _____ .

2. According to the instructions, what is difficult about choosing the categories?

   It is difficult _____ .

3. Why is the five-letter key word chosen?

   The five-letter key word is chosen _____

   _____ .

4. Why do you think a time limit is set in this game?

   In this game, a time limit is set _____

   _____ .

Exercise C

For each set of words below, create sentences about parlour games using *to + base* verbals.

1. parlour / room / used / entertain guests

   _____

2. people / parlour games / relax

   _____

3. in Charades / try / guess mystery phrases

   _____

4. playing word games / way / develop / language skills

   _____

5. difficult / play / timed games

   _____

6. score high / timed games / must / quick

   _____

One Step Beyond — Create An Activity

Exercise D

In small teams, design a parlour game and write instructions on how to play it. Include at least five *to + base* verbals in your instructions. Exchange your instructions with another team, underline the five *to + base* verbals, and play each other's game.

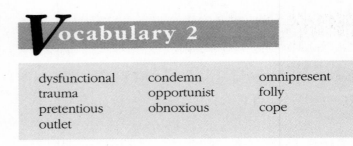

Vocabulary 2

dysfunctional	condemn	omnipresent
trauma	opportunist	folly
pretentious	obnoxious	cope
outlet		

Exercise A

From the list above, choose the four words that interest you most. Find out everything you can about these four words (their meaning, their grammatical function, their etymology (history), how often they are used, and so on). (You may have to ask an English speaker for help as you research these questions.) Be prepared to explain to your classmates why you chose these words. Maybe you think they are the most useful; perhaps there are similar words in your own language, or maybe the words just intrigue you. Once you are truly comfortable with the words, prepare to convince your classmates that they are the four best words in the list. Design an advertisement (print, audio, audio-visual, etc.) to "sell" your words. After each student has presented his or her advertisement, the class must agree on the four best words. Good luck!

Exercise B

Complete the following sentences with an appropriate form of the words from the list presented in Exercise A.

1. The _____ behaviour of some spoiled celebrities makes them unpopular with the public.

2. Playing loud music can be an _____ for expressing our own anger.

3. The _____ of an ended relationship can affect our emotional state for a long time.

4. It is _____ to think that success comes easily.

5. Many people believe that movies that encourage children to act violently should be _____ by the viewing public.

6. Television shows of the 1950s, 1960s, and 1970s created the myth of the "perfect" family in which parents and children lived peacefully together; this image was in contrast to the "real" _____ families many of us grew up in.

7. I admit that much of my good behaviour as a child was due to the belief that somehow my mother was _____ , seeing everything I did.

8. The billionaire movie producer attributes his success to his _____ approach to life.

9. The singer/songwriter was _____ in assuming she would win the music award, as there was no indication she had been chosen.

10. Marilyn Monroe's self-destructive behaviour may have been caused by her inability to _____ with the public's limited view of her talents.

One Step Beyond — Create An Activity
Exercise C

Design a vocabulary activity like the one in Unit 6, pages 92–93 of your Student Book where you create sentences with words listed in alphabetical order. Write a sentence for each of the vocabulary words used in Exercise B. Then rewrite the sentence, listing all your words in alphabetical order. Exchange your activity with a classmate. Rewrite your classmate's sentences, putting the words in logical order. Check each other's work.

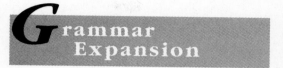

Grammar Expansion

To + base verbals (infinitives) in the perfect tense

The _to + base_ verbal is possible in the simple, progressive, and perfect forms.

simple: It's fun to watch a movie with friends.

progressive: It's fun to be watching a movie with friends.

perfect: It's fun to have watched a movie with friends.

Perfect infinitives have the same meaning as perfect or past tenses.

EXAMPLE: I'm happy _to have met_ you. (... that I met you.) = past meaning

She was sorry _to have missed_ the show. (...that she had missed the show.) = past meaning

The director expects _to have finished_ shooting the scene by noon. (...that he/she will have finished shooting...) = perfect meaning

Note: in the negative, use: _not + to + have + past participle_

EXAMPLE: I'm sorry _not to have seen_ the show.

Exercise A

Rewrite the following sentences using the perfect infinitive.

1. It appears that she didn't know the words to the song very well.

_____

_____

2. It seems that the stage actor forgot his line.

_____

_____

3. The star was disappointed that he didn't win an Academy Award.

_____

_____

4. They were sorry that they missed the first act.

_____

_____

5. The people in the audience were thrilled that they could persuade the entertainer to come out on stage for an encore.

_____

_____

6. I'm glad that I saw Céline Dion in concert last summer.

_____

_____

7. It would have been fun if I had been studying at a North American university during the goldfish-swallowing craze.

_____

_____

8. Wally and Brenda were sorry that they had missed the last episode of *The X-Files*.

_____

_____

Exercise B

Complete the following sentences with an appropriate form of the infinitive.

My husband and I had always wanted (1) _____ (see) James Taylor perform live so we were thrilled (2) _____ (learn) that he would be performing at the Molson amphitheatre in Toronto last summer. I wanted (3) _____ (be) sure (4) _____ (get) good seats so I ordered the tickets by phone the day they came on sale. On the day of the performance we wanted (5) _____ (leave for) the theatre early enough (6) _____ (avoid) traffic jams and parking nightmares. It was wonderful (7) _____ (hear) him sing some of the classics like *Fire and Rain* and *You've Got a Friend*. The concert was wonderful. We were sorry (8) _____ (wait) so long before seeing him in concert, but we were very happy (9) _____ (have) the chance to finally hear him live. And, despite the cost of the ticket, I was not at all sorry (10) _____ (spend) the money because our seats were great.

Grammar In Use

Exercise C

Elizabeth offered to plan a surprise birthday party for her friend Manuela. Below is her "To Do" list. Unfortunately, everything went wrong, and the event was a disaster. Based on this information, the list, and what went wrong with each item on the list, make deductions to complete the following sentences using infinitives.

> **To Do List**
> - send out invitations (lost in the mail?)
> - call for rental rates and book community centre hall (too expensive)
> - deliver cake to the house (the cake's icing melted in trunk of car)
> - bring pop (case left in supermarket parking lot)
> - get door prizes (stolen from car)
> - collect money from friends for gift (only raised $10)

EXAMPLE: Elizabeth meant...

> *Elizabeth meant to bring pop for the party, but she left the case in the supermarket parking lot.*

1. The invitations appear _____

_____

2. Elizabeth was not able _____

_____

3. Elizabeth intended _____

_____.

4. The door prizes seem _____

_____

5. Elizabeth had decided _____

_____

6. Elizabeth was probably sorry _____

_____

7. Manuela probably didn't expect _____

_____

8. I'm sure that Elizabeth expected _____

_____

Writing

The Essay

An essay consists of several paragraphs written about a central idea. Like paragraphs, you can write many different types of essays such as Narrative, Descriptive, Expository,

Comparison and Contrast, Classification, Process, Cause and Effect, Argumentative, and so on. The type of essay you choose will depend on your purpose for writing the essay. There are a number of common features all essays have no matter what kind they are. For example, every essay must have a title. Although essays can have as few as three, or as many paragraphs as you want, we will look at a basic five-paragraph essay. Each paragraph in the essay has a specific function.

Paragraph 1: The first paragraph serves as an introduction to the essay. It introduces the topic to be discussed, contains the thesis statement (the controlling idea of the essay), and gives some background information. In addition, it must attract the reader's attention.

Paragraphs 2-4: These are the developmental paragraphs. Depending on the type of essay being written, these main body paragraphs describe various aspects of the topic, outline causes or effects, or possibly both, indicate points of comparison or contrast, give examples, or describe processes. Each paragraph in the body has a topic sentence which clearly supports the thesis statement.

Paragraph 5: The final paragraph is the concluding paragraph. This paragraph restates or summarizes the main premise of the essay using different words than the introductory paragraph, and leaves the reader with a final thought.

Thesis Statement:
The thesis statement contains the controlling idea for the essay. It is a complete sentence and expresses a complete thought. It is similar to the topic sentence because it expresses an attitude, idea, or opinion about the topic that needs to be proved. The thesis statement is broader in scope than the topic sentence and expresses the controlling idea for the entire essay. The topic sentences contained in the body will all relate to the controlling idea in the thesis statement.

Steps to writing an effective essay
Before attempting to write an essay, it is necessary to follow some basic steps.

Step 1:   Choose a topic and narrow the topic.
Step 2:   Identify your target audience.
Step 3:   Write a thesis statement.
Step 4:   Brainstorm for ideas.
           Note: If you are not sure what aspect of the topic you really want to write about, you will need to brainstorm before you produce your thesis statement.
Step 5:   Organize your ideas into related groups and discard any that do not relate to the thesis statement.
Step 6:   Write an outline for the essay.
Step 7:   Ensure that all points on the outline support the thesis.

Step 8:   Write the first draft of your essay.
Step 9:   Revise
Step 10: Edit and give your essay a title if you don't already have one.
Step 11: Rewrite
Step 12: Proofread

The Outline
The outline, if done properly, may take you as much time to write as the actual essay; however, in the long run, it saves a lot of time and frustration. If you have carefully ensured that all your topic sentences support the thesis, that all the supporting details support the topic sentences, and there are smooth transitions between the paragraphs, you can't help but have an effective essay that is unified and coherent. Writing an essay without an outline is like building a house without a blueprint. You may know roughly how to build the house, but unless your foundations are extremely solid and your workmanship superb, you will be stuck with a problem house that will need a lot of repair — that is, if it doesn't just collapse altogether!

A skeleton outline for a five-paragraph essay would be as follows:

A. Introductory Paragraph (1)
   i) thesis statement
   ii) background information

B. Developmental (Body) Paragraphs (2,3,4)
   Paragraph 2
   i) topic sentence (a complete sentence supporting some aspect of the thesis)
   ii) supporting detail(s) (supports the topic sentence and is written in words or phrases)

   Paragraph 3
   i) topic sentence (a complete sentence supporting some aspect of the thesis)
   ii) supporting detail(s) (supports the topic sentence and is written in words or phrases)

   Paragraph 4
   i) topic sentence (a complete sentence supporting some aspect of the thesis)
   ii) supporting detail(s) (supports the topic sentence and is written in words or phrases)

C. Concluding Paragraph (5)
   i) reference to, restatement, or summary of the thesis
   ii) concluding comments

Exercise A

Read the following essay and prepare an outline of its structure by completing the chart on page 65. This essay presents a particular point of view.

The Queen of Hearts

The world was shocked on August 31, 1997, as news of the sudden death of Diana, Princess of Wales, swept across the globe. The princess died in a violent car crash early that Sunday when her speeding Mercedes limousine smashed into a pillar in a Paris underpass while fleeing from a group of paparazzi. Millions grieved and mourned her death in the weeks to follow as the world prepared for an emotional and unforgettable funeral. Her following has been likened to that of history's greats, such as Sir Winston Churchill, and to that of superstars like Marilyn Monroe. The outpouring of grief and condolences to her family — especially to her sons, princes William and Harry — was unprecedented. She was the most photographed woman in the world. Our desire to watch her every move was insatiable. Contrary to common speculation, however, it was not her beauty, her sense of fashion, her former royal title, nor her charity work that won her the hearts of the people. Diana's appeal came from a different source. Born into a world of privilege, Diana naturally radiated the grace and glamour of the world's elite, yet she displayed the human qualities of the common citizen — and therein lay her immeasurable appeal.

Unlike other public figures, Diana acknowledged her faults and this gave her a genuine human quality. She did not insist on always being portrayed in a positive light. We loved her when she was good, and we forgave her when she was bad. Diana was the good "girl-next-door." Who can forget those first images of the innocent princess in the early 1980s — head slightly bent to the side, chin tucked towards her, those shy, young eyes peeking out towards us? But Diana was also a "bad girl." She was widely criticized for spending exorbitant amounts of money on clothes. She manipulated the media during the period of her separation and divorce, and admitted to having an adulterous affair. It was precisely this good girl/bad girl image that made her appeal to others. It transformed her from the goddess Diana to the human Diana. It made her one of us.

Like us, Diana was burdened with hardships during her short life, a human quality that gave her distinct appeal. In contrast to her namesake, the goddess Diana, the hunter, Princess Diana was the hunted. She was confined by royal protocol; she was stalked by the media; and yes, she was hounded by her adoring public. The fairytale princess with the glamour, prestige, privilege, and power of the aristocrats suffered, and more importantly, she let us see how she suffered. From the child of a broken marriage, to the disdain of her mother-in-law, the queen, to the rejection of a husband who never loved her, Diana suffered at the hands of others. It is a bitter irony that even in her senseless death, Diana was being hunted as she tried to escape from the merciless paparazzi. We adored her when she was happy, and we empathized with her when she was suffering. She was, after all, one of us.

Surprisingly, the magnitude of people's suffering upon her death was immeasurable. The outpouring of grief — sincere grief — mirrored Diana's most desirable human qualities: she was sincere and compassionate. Many wives of dignitaries, politicians, and other members of the rich and famous, dutifully fulfil their role as do-gooders, jumping on the latest bandwagon of charities and causes. But with Diana we **felt** that she really cared and, as always, we **saw** that she really cared. A 1991 visit to an AIDS hospice in Toronto left the world with a winsome image of a compassionate Diana gently stroking the hands of an AIDS patient at a time when many still believed the disease could be transmitted through physical contact. When children gave her flowers, she didn't bow to them in acknowledgement as did other Royals, she knelt down to thank them at eye level. Children were her love, and her own sons were her passion. Unlike the seemingly impersonal upbringing of her former husband, Prince Charles, her own boys were raised with hugs and kisses. The princess had a heart and she gave it freely to her sons. She gave it freely to the suffering. And she gave it freely to us. She was in so many ways just like us.

Years from now when we look back in history, it will not be her charitable deeds that we remember. It will not be her beauty nor her privilege. When future generations read about Princess Diana in their history books, they will read about the unique ability she had to marry the world of the nobility and the common citizen. They will read that the people of the world loved her because through her they perceived the noble to be a little more human, and themselves to be a little more noble. They will read that Princess Diana was the people's "Queen of Hearts."

THE ESSAY

TITLE

INTRODUCTION
Thesis Statement:

BODY
Developmental Paragraph 1
Topic Sentence:

Support:

Developmental Paragraph 2
Topic Sentence:

Support:

Developmental Paragraph 3
Topic Sentence:

Support:

CONCLUSION
Topic Sentence:

Concluding Idea:

Exercise B

If you were given an assignment to write about the general topic of Popular Culture, your first step would be to narrow the topic. Fill in the circles to narrow down possible essay topics.

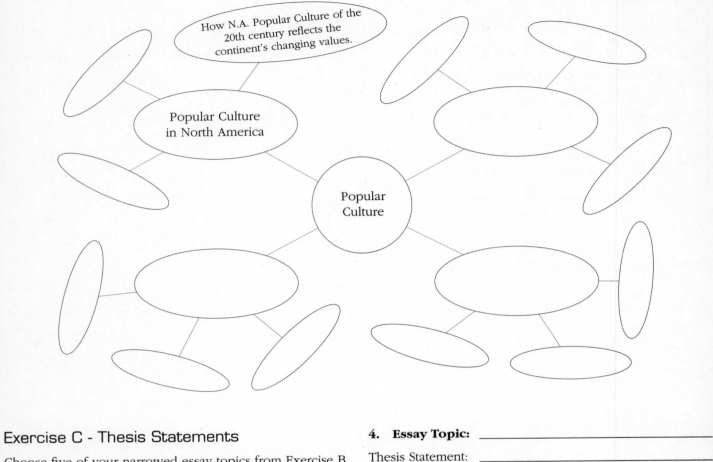

Exercise C - Thesis Statements

Choose five of your narrowed essay topics from Exercise B and write a thesis statement for each one.

1. **Essay Topic:** _____

   Thesis Statement: _____
   _____
   _____

2. **Essay Topic:** _____

   Thesis Statement: _____
   _____
   _____

3. **Essay Topic:** _____

   Thesis Statement: _____
   _____
   _____

4. **Essay Topic:** _____

   Thesis Statement: _____
   _____
   _____

5. **Essay Topic:** _____

   Thesis Statement: _____
   _____
   _____

Exercise D — Planning the Essay

Write a point-form outline for an essay on one of your topics from Exercise C.

Exercise E

Based on your outline in Exercise D, write an essay.

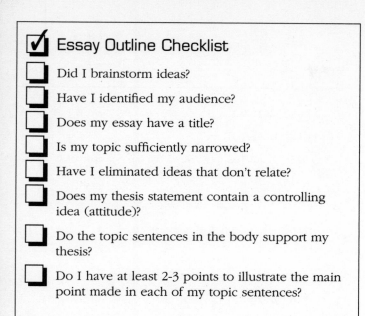

☑ Essay Outline Checklist

☐ Did I brainstorm ideas?

☐ Have I identified my audience?

☐ Does my essay have a title?

☐ Is my topic sufficiently narrowed?

☐ Have I eliminated ideas that don't relate?

☐ Does my thesis statement contain a controlling idea (attitude)?

☐ Do the topic sentences in the body support my thesis?

☐ Do I have at least 2-3 points to illustrate the main point made in each of my topic sentences?

UNIT 8
It's How You Play the Game

Exercise A

Match the idioms in Column A with their definitions in Column B.

Column A	Column B
1. ballpark figure	a. getting worse and worse
2. beat me to the punch	b. acting tough
3. bounce a few ideas off you	c. deal with a difficult situation
4. clear sailing	d. do something before I get a chance to do it
5. going downhill	e. no problems in sight
6. go the distance	f. equal in a race
7. neck and neck	g. to try something difficult
8. playing hardball	h. tell you something in order to get your opinion
9. to tackle	i. approximate value
10. wrestle with the hard facts	j. able to finish what you start

Exercise B

Complete the following dialogue using the idioms from Exercise A.

Ray: Annie, I'd like to (a) _____ you.

Annie: What's on your mind Ray? Are you thinking about the possibility that we might lose the farm?

Ray: Actually, I was thinking about baseball. I want to build a diamond in our backyard. It would be a big job (b) _____ , but something is telling me it's the right thing to do.

Annie: Are you crazy? The bank is about to foreclose on our mortgage. They are really (c) _____ . They've already told you if you don't come up with the back payments within two months, they'll take the farm from us.

Ray: Look, I know that since we moved here it has not all been (d) _____ for us. I have a gut feeling that things are going to work out for us even though it looks like it's all (e) _____ at this point. Your support would really mean a lot to me.

Annie: Give me a (f) _____ — how much would this dream of yours set us back?

Ray: About five grand by the time I add the bleachers and the lights.

Annie: Ray, I think it's time you (g) _____ . We can't even afford this farm, let alone sinking $5000 we don't have into a baseball field in the middle of nowhere.

Ray: Annie — trust me. There's a voice in my head telling me that if I build it they will come.

Annie: Who will come? I think you've finally gone off the deep end.

Ray: Trust me Annie. (h) _____ with me and you will see — they will come.

Exercise C

Gita is a camp counsellor this summer. She has been put in charge of the sports program because she said that she knew a lot about sports. Her first task is to pick up the equipment the camp will need for the various activities. The wholesaler where she is purchasing the items has everything in the back warehouse so Gita must ask specifically for everything she wants. Gita's problem is that although she knows what the equipment looks like or what it is used for, she can never remember the actual names of the items. Identify the items that Gita is trying to purchase. Identify the three sports that Gita will play at the camp this summer.

1. I guess I'll need eight of those webbed things. You know — the ones with the flat round head on a long thin handle. We're not professionals so nylon strings will be okay. _____

2. Do you carry those leather hand covers used to catch those round things? I'll need 18 right-handed ones and two left-handed ones._____

3. I'd better take two of those round leather things you blow up with the pump. All that kicking gives them quite a beating. I guess the official European size would be the best. _____

4. Please give me a half dozen of those smooth long wooden sticks. Maybe I'd better take a dozen in case a few of them get cracked if someone hits hard. Better yet, do you have any aluminum ones?_____

5. Do you carry those special covers for feet that have those points on the bottom for better traction so you don't fall when you go to kick if the grass is wet? Actually, I'll have to wait to get those because I don't know what sizes to buy. _____

6. I'll need at least a dozen of those cone-shaped things with the rubber tips. How much more are the ones that have real feathers than the ones made of plastic?

_____

Sports: 1. _____ 2. _____

3. _____

One Step Beyond – Create an Activity

Exercise D

You have the same job as Gita, but like Gita, you don't know the names of the equipment. Choose at least two sports you will play at your camp, and write descriptions for at least ten pieces of equipment. Bring the descriptions to class and exchange them with a classmate. Try to name the equipment described and determine the sport being played.

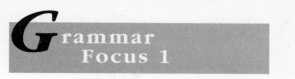

Grammar Focus 1

BASE + ING VERBALS

Exercise A

Complete the following with a gerund or gerund phrase.

1. I really regret not _____
2. He has always avoided _____
3. We discussed _____
4. As a teenager, I disliked not _____
5. Did they mention _____
6. Soccer players have to practise _____
7. I can't imagine not _____
8. Star athletes can't risk _____

Exercise B

Use verbs that are followed by gerunds such as *imagine, keep, can't help, understand, suggest, don't agree*, in order to express your opinion about the following statements.

EXAMPLE: With all the improvements in equipment, hockey is a very safe sport to play.

I can't help wondering why so many players still lose their front teeth.

1. All sports are elitist because only people with money can afford to play them.

_____

_____

2. Professional wrestling is a true sport, and not a lot of overacting as many people believe.

_____

_____

3. Girls and boys should not take part in mixed teams.

_____

_____

4. Individual sports are more challenging than team sports.

_____

_____

5. Many people do not consider that synchronized swimming is a sport that should be in the Olympics.

_____

_____

Exercise C

Change the infinitives of purpose in the following sentences to a *by + gerund* phrase.

EXAMPLE: Professional tennis players practise their serves daily to improve their accuracy.

Professional tennis players improve their accuracy *by practising their serves daily*.

1. The figure skater sharpened his skates to increase his speed.

2. Bailey ran the fastest race of his life to win the Olympic 100 m dash.

3. Ken changed the wax on his skis to accommodate the changing snow conditions.

4. Michael Chang restrung his racquet to ensure it was in top shape.

5. The baseball player caught a fly ball to end the game.

6. Chandra bowled a perfect game to win the tournament.

Exercise D

Join the following sentences by beginning each new sentence with the words in italics.

EXAMPLE: Physical sports like tennis build cardio endurance. *Tennis is appropriate for* this.

Tennis is appropriate for building cardio endurance.

1. Ken isn't sure he'll be able to afford his son's hockey equipment. *Ken is concerned about* this.

2. I'm going to Wimbledon to watch the tennis finals. *I'm very excited about* this.

3. Eric Lindros scores a lot of goals. *He is very good at* it.

4. She has the most medals for rowing won by any Canadian. *Marnie McBean is really proud of* that.

5. Kids enjoy climbing and playing on the new playground equipment. *The new jungle gym is very suitable for* that.

6. Juan and Kalil always argue when they play tennis. *They are tired of* this.

7. They must win the next game to make the playoffs. *The team is worried about* it.

8. Liam can't dive from the high board. *He's afraid of* it.

Exercise E

Fill in the blanks with a preposition + gerund.

1. This summer I am planning ____ _____ swimming at least three times a week.

2. Instead ____ _____ at home to watch TV, I plan to be more active.

3. I'm looking forward ____ _____ a little weight and getting into better shape.

4. I'm not good ____ _____ to exercise plans. I usually give up after a week.

5. In spite ____ _____ in the past, I'm going to give it my best shot.

Exercise F

Join the following sentences by beginning each new sentence with the words in italics.

EXAMPLE: They were playing tennis. That's how *we left them*.

    We left them playing tennis.

1. The park attendant likes draining the wading pool half an hour early. *We can't have him* doing that.

   _____

   _____

2. The referee is constantly making calls in favour of the other team. *I resent* that.

   _____

   _____

3. Jolene is playing at the top of her game during this tournament. *Everyone appreciates* that.

   _____

   _____

4. The neighbourhood children like playing road hockey on our street. *I don't mind them* doing that.

   _____

   _____

5. Shari is giving them swimming lessons. *They appreciate her* doing that.

   _____

   _____

Exercise G

Complete the following passage with an appropriate verbal form of five of the following verbs: *return, plan, reward, swim, dive, dart, excite, hope*. Identify the types of verbals.

I went scuba diving on the Great Barrier Reef, (a) _____ to see lots of colourful tropical fish. Luckily there were plenty of beautiful fish (b) _____ back and forth. (c) _____ on the Reef was definitely one of the highlights of my vacation in Australia. Being able to photograph the fish was (d) _____ . I plan on (e) _____ there on my next vacation.

Grammar In Use
Exercise H

Look at the following points about the benefits and disadvantages of choosing either golf or tennis as your sports activity of choice.

Tennis
- needs only a racquet and tennis balls to play
- must be played with a partner or group of four
- requires a certain amount of physical fitness and endurance
- is a fast-paced sport requiring total concentration
- allows no socializing time while playing
- competitive games are only possible when playing against someone of equal ability
- requires many areas of athletic ability: speed, hand-eye coordination, strategy, strength, endurance, etc.
- provides physical and cardio benefits

Golf
- requires golf clubs, balls and tees (Golf clubs can be rented.)
- can be played without a partner or group
- accommodates any physical characteristics of the athlete
- allows people to slow down and think about other things
- allows players to socialize while playing
- allows poor players to play competitively against good players because of the handicap system
- provides a leisurely walk and no real physical strain

Using the information above, complete the following sentences with gerund phrases.

EXAMPLE: People who have busy, stressful jobs enjoy _____

    People who have busy, stressful jobs enjoy playing golf because it allows them to relax.

1. If a tennis player enjoys a competitive game, she should avoid _____

   _____

2. People who are not in good physical shape should avoid _____

3. Golf is for people who enjoy _____

   _____

4. Tennis is for people who enjoy _____

   _____

5. Golf is for people who dislike _____

   _____

6. Tennis is for people who dislike _____

   _____

7. Tennis players are interested in _____
_____

8. Golf players are interested in _____
_____

9. Tennis players can take advantage of _____
_____

10. Golf players can take advantage of _____
_____

One Step Beyond –
Create An Activity
Exercise I

Create a questionnaire to administer to at least five different people of different age groups. Survey their likes and dislikes about sports on TV and sports they like to participate in. Compile the statistics from your survey and write at least ten sentences about the results, using gerunds or gerund phrases. Leave a blank for the gerund and exchange your exercise with a classmate.

EXAMPLE: Children detest _____ golf on TV

with their parents. Answer: having to watch

Vocabulary 2 Expansion

Exercise A

Match the sports verbs in Column A with the definitions in Column B.

Column A	Column B
1. slice	a. to hit the golf ball so it veers to one side
2. dribble	b. to hit lightly
3. slap	c. to throw the ball in the basket with force
4. slam	d. to yell and scream
5. pop (up)	e. to express disapproval or disappointment
6. groan	f. to move the ball forward by bouncing it
7. smash	g. to kick
8. roar	h. to hit up high but not very far
9. boot	i. to hit directly and straight
10. tap	j. to hit very hard

Exercise B

Complete the following spidermaps with verbs that are associated with the sport identified in the centre. Look in the sports section of the newspaper, a sports magazine, sports web pages on the Internet, or listen to a sports commentary on TV or on the radio for possible words.

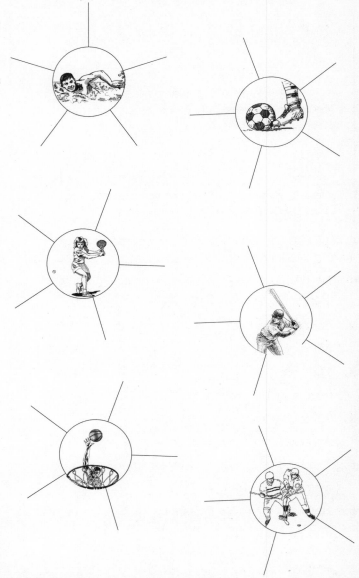

Exercise C

Write a sentence about each sport using at least one of the verbs associated with the sport that you identified in Exercise B.

Exercise D

Although many sports have different words associated with them that describe certain actions or objects, if a precise word does not exist, adjectives can be used to show the degree of intensity. Insert the following intensifiers in the chart below.

very	a bit	quite
reasonably	slightly	extremely
really	kind of	a touch
rather	a little	sort of
somewhat	pretty	awfully
substantially	much	considerably

Degree of Intensity	Intensifiers
A small degree	
A moderate degree	
A large degree	

Exercise E

Complete the following sentences by adding an appropriate intensifier.

1. Jamil is _____ out of shape. He hasn't been able to exercise since his accident a month ago.

2. Carter hit the ball _____ hard. It went right out of the park.

3. The crowd was _____ subdued. The home team was in a real slump.

4. The putt was _____ short of the hole. Another few centimetres and he would have birdied.

5. Ken has _____ improved his game since taking lessons from a pro.

6. Helga is _____ talented but not enough to turn professional.

rammar
Focus 2

GERUNDS VS. INFINITIVES

Exercise A

In the following sets of sentences, the infinitive verbal used in the first sentence is used as an *ing* verbal in the second sentence. Complete the sentences using the appropriate verb forms.

EXAMPLE: Sarin thinks it's essential to practise her backhand. She thinks __practising__ will give her a better return.

1. I hope to row in the Olympics. I really have no hope of _____ there.

2. I plan to go to the park this afternoon. _____ to the park is a great way to meet other parents with kids who enjoy outdoor activities.

3. Martin finds it interesting _____ baseball hats. He's always been interested in collecting baseball hats.

4. Ali plans to play basketball tonight despite his injury. He plans on _____ unless the doctor tells him he can't.

5. Babar was not content to win the silver medal. He would only be content after _____ the gold.

6. Jamie is excited _____ the Olympic athletes in person. He is excited about seeing their actual size.

Exercise B

For each item pictured below, write a sentence using the verb in parentheses followed by a gerund or infinitive.

EXAMPLE: (stop)

He stopped exercising months ago.

1.   (remember)

_____

2.   (forget)

_____

3.   (stop)

_____

4.   (regret)

_____

5. (remember)

_____

6. (forgot)

_____

Exercise C

Use the questions found on page 123 in the Student Book (Gerund or Infinitive?) to help you complete the following exercise. Use the list of verbs below to complete the following passage and then complete the five statements that follow, using information from the passage.

train	qualify	take part
participate	follow	perform
consider	hire	stand

(a) _____ in the Olympics must be an incredible thrill. As we watch the events on television, we often forget (b) _____ the months, if not years, of practice that have taken place in order for the athletes (c) _____ on the podium representing their country. They have sacrificed their social lives and family time (d) _____ a gruelling (e) _____ schedule. Considerable expense has gone into (f) _____ the best coaches. The (g) _____ tournaments leading up to this final shot at the gold have given the athletes practice (h) _____ their sport in front of large crowds, but nothing can compare to the Olympics themselves. In the end, only three individuals or groups will stand on those podiums, but one must keep in mind that everyone who gets (i) _____ in the Olympics is a winner.

1. Olympic athletes can't stop _____

2. It is very expensive _____

3. _____ is a thrill of a lifetime.

4. It is important _____

5. The athletes follow a _____

Grammar In Use

Exercise D

Underline at least eight infinitive or *ing* verbals in the following passage.

Athletes keep getting better every year with the improvement of training facilities and equipment. Existing world records are broken on a regular basis. Many athletes, desperate to win the glory of the gold, turn to performance-enhancing drugs such as steroids and other forms of hopefully untraceable drugs. Regular drug testing of athletes is now a requirement in the highly competitive world of athletics. The number of these records that have been awarded to athletes who have managed to slip by the testing is unclear. However, what remains a little changed fact is the average age of top-performing athletes. In the early 1900s, the average age of gold medal winners was 25. Today, this average has changed only slightly to 24.6. This indicates that no matter what athletes do to improve their training, equipment or performance, age will probably be the most influential factor.

Based on the information in the paragraph, complete the following sentences with a logical verbal or verbal phrase.

1. Athletes are determined _____

2. _____ is an illegal way to enhance performance.

3. Many athletes are desperate _____

4. Officials are forced _____

5. Athletes are willing to risk _____

One Step Beyond – Create An Activity

Exercise E

Find a short, interesting article in the sports section of a newspaper or magazine. Rewrite the article leaving a blank for every verbal. At the bottom of the article, write at least five questions which require a verbal in the answer. Exchange your exercise with a classmate.

Writing

Introductory Paragraphs

The introduction of an essay is generally one paragraph. The paragraph introduces the topic to be developed in the rest of the essay. It contains the thesis statement, background information, and indicates how the topic will be developed. Therefore, the introductory paragraph will indicate the kind of essay you are writing (descriptive, narrative, cause and effect, process, comparison and contrast, etc.). It is important that the introductory paragraph contain information that the reader will find interesting or intriguing so the reader will want to continue to read the rest of the essay. It is not advisable to open the essay with the thesis because providing an opinion immediately does not necessarily entice the reader to read on. There are four main approaches that writers use when writing an introductory paragraph.

1) **Attention Grabber:** Start the essay with a very interesting example pertinent to the topic.

2) **Quotation:** Start the essay with an interesting quotation that relates to the topic.

3) **Opposite:** Start the essay with a statement that is actually contrary to the thesis.

4) **Cone:** Start the essay with general details and then progress to specific points.

Exercise A

Look at the following introductory paragraphs. Identify the paragraph that contains all the items in the Introductory Paragraph Checklist at the end of this unit.

1. Many new sports are being added to the Olympics regularly. Despite recent controversy, sports such as bowling and synchronized swimming have been added to the games. This isn't a good idea in my opinion.

2. You really have to be a non-socializing introvert to want to dedicate yourself totally to becoming the best at a sport. Long hours of practice take up the time you would normally be spending with friends. Casual dates and get-togethers are impossible, especially before gruelling schedules. Athletes have the chance to meet many people from all over the world at tournaments. They become champions in their local communities, often visiting local schools to promote sports and hard work. Athletes are dedicated individuals who usually positively influence people around them with their community service and dedication to the sport.

3. In an event unprecedented in professional wrestling, Mike Tyson bit Evander Hollyfield's ear, bringing the match, and his career, to a stunning end. What new low has professional athletics been dragged down to when boxers, earning millions of dollars for ten rounds in a ring, whether they win or not, temporarily lose it and turn into animals? Was it the pressure of the media hype surrounding the match? Was it a case of temporary insanity in which he totally lost control? Was it consciously done in the hopes that somehow he might win? No matter what the cause, Tyson's disgraceful behaviour cannot be tolerated or forgiven.

4. "I didn't take any drugs," Ben Johnson said, as the medal was stripped from him. The adamant denial of wrongdoing gave Canada a glimmer of hope. As the day passed, and the tests were verified, the disgraceful truth was confirmed. Another athlete had used steroids to enhance his performance. The honeymoon that Ben Johnson briefly enjoyed with Canada was over, as a nation hung its head in shame.

Exercise B

Look at paragraph 3 in Exercise A. Identify the following:

1. Thesis statement _____

2. Approach _____

3. Background Info _____

4. Kind of Essay (rhetorical mode) _____

5. Point of view (controlling idea) _____

Exercise C

1. Write a thesis statement for each of the following topics.

2. Write introductory paragraphs using the thesis statements. Use a different approach for each paragraph.

   a. The major changes in the Olympics in the last 100 years.
   b. Olympic athletes: professionals or amateurs?
   c. Drugs and sports
   d. The glory of the gold

Use the Introductory Paragraph Checklist to ensure your paragraph is complete.

✓ Introductory Paragraph Checklist

☐ Will the paragraph get the reader's attention?

☐ Does the paragraph contain a thesis statement which indicates the point of view of the writer?

☐ Does the paragraph use one of the four main approaches: attention grabber, quotation, opposite, cone?

☐ Does the introductory paragraph provide some background information?

☐ Does the introductory paragraph indicate the kind of essay that will be developed?

UNIT 9
Food For Thought

Vocabulary 1

interloper	tread	atmosphere
perishable	impulse	unique
onslaught	enticement	govern
diversification		

Exercise A

Complete the following sentences with a form of the vocabulary words listed above.

1. Her _____ behaviour amused her friends but worried her parents.

2. Despite valiant efforts on behalf of the firefighters, two people _____ in the fire.

3. The _____ pressure is making my head ache.

4. Her _____ outlook on life makes her a very interesting person to be with.

5. The _____ against government cutbacks has never been witnessed in this country before.

6. The _____ came in, interrupted the meeting, gave his unwanted opinion and left.

7. Helga has such a heavy _____ that she could wake the dead if she walked across their graves.

8. The _____ has been creating some very unpopular policies lately.

9. Our investment manager suggested that we _____ our portfolio to ensure we don't risk everything on one stock.

10. All the candies placed at the supermarket checkout are there to _____ children to want junk food.

Exercise B

The $2500 Dollar Pyramid
Each block of the pyramid below has a list of words or phrases on it which relate to a form of the vocabulary words from Listening 1 (Before You Listen #3) on page 133 in the Student Book. Award yourself the monetary value for each correct word you guess. Then write a sentence for each of the answers that demonstrates your understanding of the word.

EXAMPLE:

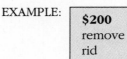

$200
remove
rid
undesirable

Answer: Things that relate to "purge"

F. $900
food
drink
alive

D. $500
manage
handle
deal with

E. $500
urge
uncontrollable
driven by desire

A. $200
drugs
caffeine
cigarettes

B. $200
overweight
unhealthy
very fat

C. $200
excessive
spree
eating frenzy

Exercise C – Expansion Activity

Fill in the blanks in the reading with the following words.

benefits	emerged	prevailing
substance	declares	counterproductive
wiser	secretion	dosage
nutrition		

Nutrition Council Grapples With Conflicting Advice

Everyday, it seems, a new headline (a) _____ that this food is good for you, that food is bad for you, and another food turns out not to do what you thought it was going to when you were gulping it down.

What's a consumer to do?

The 3000 nutritionists, dieticians and researchers who are gathered in Montreal this week at the International Congress of Nutrition may be able to answer that question. In 152 papers and hundreds of poster displays, they are offering up food for thought, and thoughts about food, that with any luck will help people make (b)_____ choices at the grocery store.

"(c) _____ is a popular topic, and more and more so, but everybody has become an expert, and that makes it more and more difficult for nutritionists," said Louise Lambert-Lagacé, president of the conference and an oft-cited author on nutrition.

But claims about the health (d) _____ of certain foods can have more weight when they come from the mouth of a scientist than from the back of a cereal box, she suggested.

That is not to say that the research discussed at the conference is free of controversy. Walter Willett, head of the nutrition department at Harvard, attracted attention Monday by challenging the (e) _____ orthodoxy that fat makes us fat.

The saturated fat in dairy products and meat isn't so bad for the waistline, he said: It's the trans-fatty acids in hydrogenated oils that add pounds. A diet low in fat and high in carbohydrates is probably (f) _____ , in his view.

Many of the studies discussed at the conference are not accessible. "OB protein: the link between adiposity and central neural networks" is not the sort of thing that easily trickles down to kitchen table conversations. But the basic science that has the researchers excited may eventually be of use to ordinary people trying to figure out what to eat or feed to their children.

Some of the research in that regard that has (g) _____ from the conference so far: Nutritionists, who have long touted the benefits of a fibre-rich diet, may have one more reason to urge us to eat more whole-grain cereals and breads, fruits and vegetables. A high-fibre diet can condition the body to produce more

insulin, which may allow those Type 2 (adult-onset) diabetics who take insulin to take less of it or reduce their (h) _____ of pancreas-stimulating drugs, said Michael McBurney, a researcher at the University of Alberta.

According to Dr. McBurney's research, dietary fibre fermenting in the intestine stimulates the (i) _____ of a hormone that travels to the pancreas, which in turn releases insulin, the (j) _____ that controls blood sugar. The results could be seen in animal experiments after two weeks of a high-fibre diet, Dr. McBurney said. For humans, high fibre means an average of 25 grams a day; most Canadians get only 10 to 15 grams.

Glossary
oft-cited – quoted often
orthodoxy – widely accepted belief
trans-fatty acid – naturally-occurring fats and oils
hydrogenated – combined or treated with hydrogen
carbohydrates – substances such as sugar or starch
adiposity – a tendency to become fat
neural – relating to a nerve or nervous system
trickles – makes its way slowly
touted – offered in the hope that people will accept it
fermenting – changing state due to a chemical reaction caused by yeast or bacteria
pancreas – a gland that produces substances which help break down food

Exercise D – Quiz

"Old wives' tales" are sayings that are passed down from generation to generation. They are supposed to provide guidance; however, some of these sayings are true and can be helpful, while others are completely false. There are countless "tales" that are related to food. Read the following "tales" and indicate if you think they are true [T] or false [F].

1. You'll get zits (pimples) if you eat too much chocolate or fried food.

2. Chicken soup is good medicine for a cold.

3. Wearing a clove of garlic around your neck will prevent you from getting sick.

4. Put a steak on a black eye.

5. If you have an upset stomach, eat crackers, drink flat gingerale, or eat ginger.

6. Breakfast is the most important meal of the day.

7. Carrots are good for your eyesight.

8. Brown eggs are more nutritious than white eggs.

9. Don't eat between meals; you'll spoil your appetite.

10. Brown sugar, raw sugar, molasses, and honey are healthier than refined white sugar.

One Step Beyond – Create An Activity

Exercise E

Create an activity similar to Exercise D using "old wives' tales" or other "stories" you are familiar with from your culture.

BASE + D/T/N VERBALS

Exercise A

Complete the following sentences using the appropriate verbal form in parentheses. Note that you will need to use some *base + ing* verbals.

1. It's a _____ (well-know) fact that many children do not eat a healthy breakfast before going to school.

2. These _____ (fat-reduce) brownies taste almost as good as the regular ones.

3. Jane's _____ (all-consume) passion for rich foods has led to many health problems.

4. Do you really think that this _____ (weight-reduce) cream works?

5. The _____ (well-train) diet expert can identify healthful food products at a glance.

6. I find _____ (confuse) product labels very frustrating.

7. The _____ (frequently mention) fact that eating fat makes you fat is really a fallacy.

8. It was _____ (disappoint) to discover that my favourite sandwich was full of calories.

9. There are many _____ (prepackage) foods on the market that are both nutritious and low-calorie.

10. Unfortunately, there are many _____ (hide) calories in supposedly healthful foods.

Exercise B

Rewrite the following sentences so that they are more concise.

EXAMPLE: Jean has a cupboard full of fruit that has been canned.
Jean has a cupboard full of **canned** fruit.

1. Top athletes follow diets that have been carefully planned.

_____

_____

2. Kate Moss, who has been much-photographed, looks anorexic.

_____

_____

3. The statistics, which are frightening, indicate that death due to eating disorders is on the rise amongst teenagers.

_____

_____

4. My mother, who was well-intentioned, told me to watch my weight.

_____

_____

5. The debate on nutrition that was televised was insightful.

_____

_____

6. The results, which were surprising, made headlines around the world.

_____

_____

Exercise C

Read the following newspaper article written about the labeling of foods. Underline at least eight examples of *base + d/t/n* verbals.

78

Foods That Harm, Foods That Heal

Because of a clause in the Canada-US Free Trade Agreement, which requires the two countries to work toward an equivalent labeling system, food labels in Canada are likely to change in the near future. At the
5 present time, the only label requirement on processed foods is a list of ingredients in descending order by weight. The label also includes the name and address of the manufacturer, packager, or distributor, the packaging date, or the last date on which it can be sold or
10 consumed, plus storage information. Nutritional information, now optional, will probably be mandatory when the new policies and regulations are enacted. Canada's plan is to show serving sizes, the number of servings in a package, and the calories per serving at
15 the top of the label, in much the same way as the United States currently does.

The United States has established standard serving sizes for each type of food, regardless of brand. This is a departure from its practices in the past, when one
20 brand might specify a serving as half a cup, and another brand's serving would be one cup. The new method is especially helpful to people who are watching their weight or who are on special diets. The Canadian plan is to match the American serving sizes
25 in virtually all cases.

The new Canadian food label will simplify the breakdown of nutrients in a food, listing the grams contained in the five key categories: total fat and amount of saturated fat; cholesterol; sodium; carbohydrates,
30 including sugars and fibre; and protein. Also, the percentage of Recommended Nutrient Intakes (RNIs) that these amounts represent will be shown. The label may also list the major vitamins and minerals, along with the percentage of RNI. Canada may follow the Amer-
35 ican lead which currently states the recommended amounts of carbohydrates, protein, and dietary fibre in diets that permit 2000 and 2500 calories a day.

Setting a Standard

Proposed Canadian regulations aim to set standards for
40 terms such as "light/lite" or "low-fat". For example, a food that normally derives more than 50% of its calories from fat can be marketed in a "light" version, only if the fat content has been reduced by more than one-third. "Light" will also be allowed to describe char-
45 acteristics such as flavour, texture, or colour, but the connection must be identified as in "light in flavour". Unlike the United States, Canada will not permit "light" in reference to nutrients such as sodium. Health claims are allowed as long as they are based on evidence
50 accepted by qualified experts. Claims such as "calorie-reduced," "low-fat" and "low cholesterol," may be used as long as they conform to regulations. For example, calorie-reduced means that a food has 50% fewer calories than the regular version. Low cholesterol
55 means there can be no more than 3 mg per serving, and the food must be low in saturated fat.

Exercise D

Complete the following sentences with a *base + d/t/n* verbal or *base + ing* verbal. Use a form of the following base verbs: *simplify, influence, package, recommend, concern, utilize, approve, face, establish, inform*.

1. _____ about misleading or incomplete labels, the originators of the Canada-US Free Trade Agreement have included a clause requiring equivalent labeling.

2. Previously, _____ labels contained the list of ingredients in descending order by weight, the name and address of the manufacturer, the _____ date or best before date, as well as storage information.

3. _____ standards in the US will probably serve as a guideline for labeling nutritional information.

4. A _____ breakdown in nutrients will lead to better _____ consumers.

5. _____ regulations will standardize terms such as light/lite and low fat.

6. Dieticians hope that people, _____ by the information on the labels, will eat in a more healthful way.

7. Manufacturers, _____ with strict guidelines on the use of words such as "light" and "calorie-reduced" will have to change their marketing strategy.

8. Labels, _____ correctly, could help improve the health of many North Americans.

Exercise E

Identify the "function" of the verbals in Exercise D, for example, pre-modifier, post-modifier, etc.

Grammar In Use
Exercise F

Our relationship with food is often closely related to our emotional state. For example, when bored, some people tend to eat junk food. Some people are bored during lectures, while watching TV, or simply sitting around the house. Complete the following chart.

Emotions	Situations that make me feel that way	How I react when I feel that way	Foods I eat when I feel that way
relaxed			
interested			
excited			
worried			
frustrated			

Now write ten sentences describing the results you recorded in the chart.

EXAMPLE: When I'm bored, I eat junk food.

I find documentaries boring so I usually go and get some popcorn.

Vocabulary 2

Exercise A

Reread the article on page 79 earlier. Circle all the words you find with the following suffixes: *-ly, -al, -ion, -er.* Insert the words in the chart below and then complete the chart by writing in other forms of the words where possible.

suffix	noun	verb	adjective	adverb
-ly				
-al				
-ion				
-er				

Exercise B

Complete the following word maps with words formed by adding suffixes to the bases in the circles. Then write a sentence for each word to show your understanding of the meaning.

EXAMPLE: **diet** — dietician

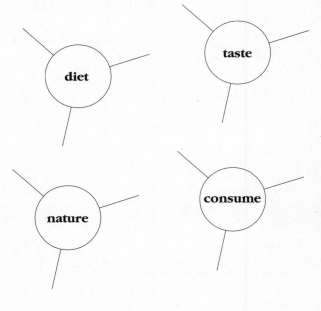

One Step Beyond – Create An Activity

Exercise C

List the words you selected in Exercise B in Column A, and write definitions for these words in random order in Column B. Exchange your work with a classmate and complete each other's activity.

 **riting**

Body Paragraphs

In a five-paragraph essay, the body paragraphs are paragraphs 2-4. Each paragraph addresses one aspect of support for the attitude expressed in the thesis. Each paragraph contains a topic sentence that supports the thesis statement and controls the direction of the paragraph. It is very important to link the paragraphs so that the essay is smooth and coherent. This is done through transitional sentences which are usually the first or last sentence of the paragraph. The exact contents of the body paragraphs will depend on the type of essay being written. The paragraphs should be presented logically, in order of importance, in order of familiarity, or in time order.

Exercise A

One way to determine the topics for the body paragraphs is to turn the thesis statement into a question and then brainstorm possible answers to the question. Each paragraph in the body can address a different answer to the question.

EXAMPLE: **Thesis:** Eating disorders amongst teens have been increasing at an unacceptable rate in the last decade.

Question: Why have eating disorders amongst teens been increasing at an unacceptable rate in the last decade?

Answers: 1. media portrayal of thin being best
2. need for acceptance
3. low self-esteem

Change the following thesis statements into questions and provide three possible answers to each question.

1. **Thesis:** The best solution to the hunger crisis in developing countries would be one they develop themselves.

   Question: _____

   _____

   Answers:

   1) _____

   _____

   2) _____

   _____

   3) _____

   _____

2. **Thesis:** Food banks do not solve the chronic hunger problems of the city's poor.

   Question: _____

   _____

   Answers:

   1) _____

   _____

   2) _____

   _____

   3) _____

   _____

3. **Thesis:** Education about healthful living and eating is the key to an improved lifestyle.

   Question: _____

   _____

   Answers:

   1) _____

   _____

   2) _____

   _____

   3) _____

   _____

Exercise B

The topic sentence of each paragraph must support one aspect of the thesis statement.

EXAMPLE: **Thesis:** Eating disorders amongst teens have increased in the last decade.

Possible topic sentences:

1) The media portrayal of "thin being best" has brainwashed teens to think that if they aren't thin they aren't socially acceptable.

2) Teens' need for acceptance by their peers has contributed to eating disorders.

3) Teens' low self-esteem has led to cases of anorexia and bulimia.

Now rewrite the topics [Answers 1), 2), 3)] from Exercise A into topic sentences.

1. **Thesis:** The best solution to the hunger crisis in developing countries would be one they develop themselves.

Topic Sentences:

1) _____
   _____

2) _____
   _____

3) _____

2. Thesis: Food banks do not solve the chronic hunger problems of the city's poor.

Topic Sentences:

1) _____
   _____

2) _____
   _____

3) _____
   _____

3. Thesis: Education about healthful living and eating is the key to an improved lifestyle.

Topic Sentences:

1) _____
   _____

2) _____
   _____

3) _____
   _____

EXAMPLE: **Possible transitions:**

1) Social acceptance amongst teens is very important to them.

2) Teens who do not feel accepted by their peers often suffer from low self-esteem.

1. Transitions:

1) _____
   _____

2) _____
   _____

2. Transitions:

1) _____
   _____

2) _____
   _____

3. Transitions:

1) _____
   _____

2) _____
   _____

Concluding Paragraph
The final paragraph of the essay brings the essay to an end. It contains a reference to, or restatement of, the thesis statement. The final paragraph leaves the reader with some concluding thoughts, but should contain no new information.

Exercise C

Transitional sentences between paragraphs are essential to ensure a smooth, coherent essay. Consider the three topic sentences in Exercise B and write out two possible transition sentences that you could use between the paragraphs.

Thesis: Eating disorders amongst teens have increased in the last decade.

Topic Sentences:

1) The media portrayal of "thin being best" has brainwashed teens to think that if they aren't thin they aren't socially acceptable.

2) Teens' need for acceptance by their peers has contributed to eating disorders.

3) Teens' low self-esteem has led to cases of anorexia and bulimia.

Exercise D

Here is a sample concluding paragraph for the following thesis: Eating disorders amongst teens have increased in the last decade.

Conclusion:
Anorexia nervosa and bulimia are just a few of the eating disorders that have plagued teens in the last decade. The influence of media, low self-esteem, and the desperate need for social acceptance have all led to increased diet-related problems. This increase should serve as a warning that cannot be ignored.

Write sample conclusions for the three outlines developed in Exercise B.

Exercise E

Write an essay for one of the outlines developed in Exercise B or a topic of your choice. Use the following checklist to edit your work.

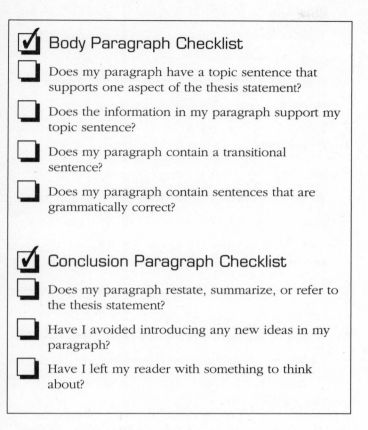

☑ Body Paragraph Checklist

☐ Does my paragraph have a topic sentence that supports one aspect of the thesis statement?

☐ Does the information in my paragraph support my topic sentence?

☐ Does my paragraph contain a transitional sentence?

☐ Does my paragraph contain sentences that are grammatically correct?

☑ Conclusion Paragraph Checklist

☐ Does my paragraph restate, summarize, or refer to the thesis statement?

☐ Have I avoided introducing any new ideas in my paragraph?

☐ Have I left my reader with something to think about?

UNIT 10
The Circle of Life

Vocabulary 1

Exercise A

Let's play a word game! The definitions below correspond to ten of the vocabulary words in the box. Ask the question "What is?" about each word from the list as you match it to a definition.

EXAMPLE: This five-syllable word is synonymous with "modern" when used as an adjective, but can also be used as a noun to mean a person who is the same age as you.

"What is *contemporary*?"

tryout	turbulent	flourishing
flaming	serene	global
revolution	apprentice	develop
mature	theory	strive
contemporary	span	resolve
evolve		

1. This word is often used to give a more formal context to the verb "decide," but it is more commonly used in the context of ending a problem or a difficulty. What is _____?

2. You will usually hear this word used to refer to the length (especially of time) between two points. In the context of cleanliness, however, you will recognize the expression "spick and _____." What is _____?

3. This person was someone who worked for low wages with a master craftsperson or other skilled worker in order to learn a trade. Add "ship" to this word and you will have a description of a very practical educational and working experience. What is _____?

4. A bit formal for everyday conversation, you are more likely to hear this verb in a speech or in formal writing. There is a noble connotation to this word that expresses a strong will to achieve. What is _____?

5. A scientist cannot live without this often-used word. Think of Einstein's famous discovery and you will guess this word relatively quickly. What is _____?

6. A gradual development could be described using this two-syllable verb. Think about the relationship between apes and humans and you're sure to find this word. What is _____?

7. You'll find this noun about three-quarters of the way through any dictionary. If you're a Beatles fan, you'll remember the first line from one of the band's hit songs from the 1960s, "You say you want a _____". If you're not a fan, you'll have to rely on the use of this word in a political context. What is _____?

8. A high school or post-secondary student who is older than the usual age is referred to as this type of student. If you still can't guess the word, remember that girls do this faster than boys. What is _____?

9. Although this common English word can be used in several contexts, you will likely hear it used as an adjective in a branch of psychology that studies how humans grow and change. What is _____?

10. Like the bumpy airplane flying through the rough weather of high winds, a relationship that has its ups and downs is referred to as a _____ relationship. What is _____?

Now use each of these ten words in a sentence that demonstrates your comprehension of its meaning.

Exercise B

For each of the following adjectives, use your dictionary or other written material to discover at least three nouns it could describe: *theoretical; global; mature; serene; contemporary*. Write sentences for the words you discover on a separate sheet of paper.

EXAMPLE: **contemporary:** art; fashion; philosophy; design; architecture

Exercise C

Read an English newspaper or magazine and look for the following words (or a form of these words): *resolve, theory, contemporary, global, development*. Write out the sentence that contains each word and be prepared to explain the context of the sentence. You're most likely to find these words in articles about business, politics, or the community.

One Step Beyond — Create An Activity

Exercise D

Design a word game activity like the one in Exercise A of Vocabulary 1 in this unit. Choose ten words from Reading 1, page 147 in your Student Book. Write clues, and then exchange your activity with a classmate.

Grammar Focus

TENSE REVIEW

Exercise A

Some of the underlined verbs in the sentences below are correct in tense and some are incorrect. Write (C) for correct or (I) for incorrect and correct the inaccuracies.

Note: Let the meaning and the tenses of other verbs in the sentence guide you.

1. Psychologists agree that age <u>played</u> an important role in how people interact with each other.

2. The stage of human development called "youth" only <u>will take on</u> its current meaning a few decades ago.

3. The "Ages-and-Stages" approach to adult development <u>had been criticized</u> because it doesn't appear to apply to women.

4. In the future, advertisers <u>have no longer targeted</u> the youth market.

5. Before the 1950s, psychologists <u>had concentrated</u> their efforts on defining the stages of childhood.

6. These days, by the time many couples get married, they <u>will likely live</u> together for at least one year.

7. People commonly believe that intellectual abilities slowly <u>deteriorated</u> with advancing age.

8. The main task of young adulthood, according to Erikson, <u>is</u> to establish love and intimacy in personal relationships.

Exercise B

Fill in the blanks with the correct tense of the verb "develop."

1. Children _____ language skills very early.

2. During the decade of the sixties, North American teens, without realizing it, _____ a new social system for young adults that would last into the next thirty years and beyond.

3. For about a year now, engineers at Alpha Computers _____ a new virtual software program that allows users to project themselves into the future.

4. Researchers _____ (just) an early detection system for this genetic disorder.

5. Now at 24, Martha _____ an interest in children.

6. Piaget _____ a comprehensive theory about human development, but it ignored adult development entirely.

7. I am certain that we _____ new ways to combat age-related diseases during the next decade.

8. Many believe that by the middle of the 21st century, science _____ a system for extending life into the 100-plus year range.

9. As you get older, you _____ memory loss.

10. The Canadian pharmaceutical industry _____ a new drug for colon cancer when Pharma AGF in Germany announced its new cancer-fighting drug.

11. Erikson _____ his theory of life stages before the 1980s.

12. By the end of this year, Longlife Insurance Company _____ its new "Retirement Freedom" product for fourteen months. The company expects to introduce the product to consumers early next year.

Exercise C

Write sentences using the following verbs in the tenses indicated in parentheses.

1. evolve (present simple) _____
   _____

2. resolve (future simple) _____
   _____

3. develop (past continuous) _____
   _____

4. mature (present perfect continuous) _____
   _____

5. strive (present continuous) _____
   _____

6. span (future continuous) _____
   _____

7. globalize (future perfect) _____
   _____

8. apprentice (past simple) _____
   _____

9. theorize (past perfect) _____
   _____

10. resolve (present perfect) _____
    _____

11. flourish (future perfect continuous) _____
    _____

12. try out (past perfect continuous) _____
    _____

Look up the word "conflict" in the dictionary and write a sentence for each of its different uses. Note that "conflict" is often associated with specific words such as the prepositions and verbs in the examples below.

EXAMPLES: to be in conflict **with** something/someone

a conflict **between** two or more things

to **come into** conflict with

to **resolve** a conflict

Now choose two or three other words from the reading "A New Look At Human Development" on page 147 of your Student Book, (for example: *divide, associate, concern*) and use a dictionary to analyze the functions, meanings, and word associations of these words.

For each word:

1. list its meanings and write a sentence for each meaning.

2. list other grammatical forms and their meanings if they differ from the meanings in point 1.

3. list other words often associated with it.

Be prepared to share your work with your classmates.

Exercise B

Match the prepositions to the verbs in the circles. Note that in some cases more than one preposition can be used with each verb.

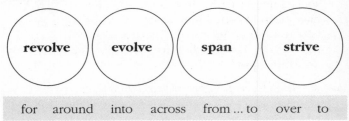

| for | around | into | across | from ... to | over | to |

Write the meaning of each word pair (verb + preposition) and write a sentence for each.

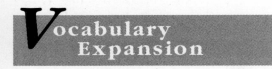

WORD INTIMACY

Exercise A

The word "conflict" is a slightly formal word and, when used as a noun, can mean an active disagreement or fight between individuals, groups, or countries. As a verb (to conflict), it can be used to suggest that one thing contradicts another. As an adjective (conflicting), it can mean things that don't fit together well because they are different.

SHIFTING TENSES

You will notice in the Student Book reading "The Cardboard Box Is Marked 'The Good Stuff'" that although we can identify a main time perspective for each paragraph, there are occasional shifts in time and consequently in tense. Normally, it is not acceptable in English to shift tenses unnecessarily. However, there are situations when it is acceptable.

It is acceptable to shift tenses when:

1. *you are giving specific examples to illustrate a general statement*

   Driven by a desire to understand human nature, physicians, philosophers, and other professionals have critically examined the motivations, challenges, and key influences in human behaviour at various key stages of human development. Critical work in this field was done at the turn of the last century by Sigmund Freud, a trained physician, who theorized that children's development could be defined in terms of psychosexual development.

2. *you are showing an important contrast in time that is clearly signalled*

   The media paint a dismal picture of our education system, suggesting that students today are not learning how to read, write, or do arithmetic as well as those in our grandparents' generation. But a study of literacy rates among different generational groups in Canada published in 1990, revealed that while almost 75% of Canadians between the ages of 16 and 34 could handle the reading requirements of daily life, only 33% of Canadians between the ages of 55 and 69 were functionally literate. This demonstrates that fewer people in our parents' and grandparents' generation had access to education. Also, while the education system is struggling to meet the needs of a diverse student body, students with special needs, who a few decades ago would never have been included in mainstream education, now benefit from an inclusive education that challenges them to live beyond their real and perceived disadvantages.

3. *you are interrupting your text with a statement of general truth*

   Grandmother didn't want to enter the nursing home despite Mother's urging. Sadly, Grandmother could no longer prepare her own meals or even wash herself. My mother, my sisters, and I took turns cleaning and cooking for Grandmother, but this was becoming increasingly stressful for our own families. Nonetheless, Grandmother simply wouldn't hear of going into a nursing home. She said that as long as she was in her own home, she had some sense of being in control. People want to be in control of their own lives — that's only natural. Grandmother finally did enter the home, but not until two years later. And those were two years she cherished.

Exercise A

In the paragraphs above, underline the sentences or clauses that show a change in time frame.

Exercise B

Helen attended a reunion of some of her colleagues at the tourist board where she worked ten years ago. Read the thank-you note she wrote to her host. Rewrite the note, putting the forms of the verbs in parentheses in an appropriate tense. (You may have to supply modals in some cases to make the meaning clear.)

Dear Barbara,

It (1) _____ (be) great to see you and the gang at the reunion last Saturday. Thanks for inviting me. I (2) _____ (not believe) how time (3) _____ (fly)! The last time I (4) _____ (see) Cathy and Bernhardt, they (5) _____ (have) no children. Now they (6) _____ (be) parents of three adorable little ones. Deborah (7) _____ (not look) a day older than when I (8) _____ (see) her ten years ago. And Ava and Steve's two children (9) _____ (look) so grown up. (10) _____ (Be) Jessica really only eleven? She (11) _____ (look) like such a young lady. It (12) _____ (seem) that only yesterday Ava (13) _____ (announce) she (14) _____ (be) pregnant with Philip. Truly, where (15) _____ (go) the time? It (16) _____ (be) great to see everyone's photos too — Karen's son Shaun with the gold medal he (17) _____ (win) for snowboarding and Jamie speed skiing. Those boys (18) _____ (be) Olympic medallists one day. You (19) _____ (believe) that Dave's daughter (20) _____ (marry) last year? She (21) _____ (be) just a child when we (22) _____ (work) at the tourist board. Before you know it our own children (23) _____ (marry) and (24) _____ (leave) the nest. Hope to see you all again before then. Thanks again for the great time.

Love,

Helen, Mike, Jacklyn, and Paul

The Town Mouse and the Country Mouse

A country mouse (1) _____ (be) very happy that

his city cousin, the town mouse, (2) _____

(accept) his invitation to dinner. He (3) _____

(give) his city cousin all the best food he

(4) _____ (have), such as dried beans, peas, and

crusts of bread. The town mouse (5) _____ (try)

not to show how he (6) _____ (dislike) the

food and (7) _____ (pick) a little here and

(8) _____ (taste) a little there to be polite. After

dinner, however, he (9) _____ (say), "How can

you (10) _____ (stand) such food all the time?

Still I (11) _____ (suppose) here in the country

you (12) _____ (not know) about any better.

Why you (13) _____ (not go) home with me?

Once you (14) _____ (taste) the delicious things

I (15) _____ (eat), you (16) _____ (never

want) to come back here." The country mouse not only

kindly (17) _____ (forgive) the town mouse for

not liking his dinner, but even (18) _____

(consent) to go that very evening to the city with his

cousin. They (19) _____ (arrive) late at night;

and the city mouse, as host, (20) _____ (take)

his country cousin at once to a room where there

(21) _____ (be) a big dinner. "You

(22) _____ (must be) tired," he (23) _____

(say). "(24) _____ (Rest) here, and I

(25) _____ (bring) you some real food." And he

(26) _____ (bring) the country mouse such things

as nuts, dates, cakes, and fruit. The country mouse

(27) _____ (think) it was all so good, he

(28) _____ (want) to stay there. But before he

(29) _____ (have) a chance to say so, he

(30) _____ (hear) a terrible roar, and looking up,

he (31) _____ (see) a huge creature dash into the

room. Frightened half out of his wits, the country

mouse (32) _____ (run)

from the table, and round

and round the room, trying to

find a hiding place. At last he

(33) _____ (find) a place

of safety. While he (34) _____

(stand) there trembling, he (35)

_____ (make) up his mind to go home as

soon as he (36) _____ (can get) safely away; for,

to himself, he (37) _____ (say) "I'd rather

(38) _____ (have) common food in safety than

dates and nuts in the midst of danger."

The troubles you know (39) _____ *(be) the*

easiest to bear.

Exercise C

Aesop's Fables are loved by millions of North American children. Read "The Town Mouse and the Country Mouse" on the previous page, filling in the blanks with an appropriate form of the verbs in parentheses. Look carefully at the context when deciding on the appropriate tense of each verb. (Tenses can change in particular situations.)

Grammar In Use
Exercise D

Write a letter to an English-speaking Canadian friend, describing how young people in your native country or region like to spend their school holidays. Give a specific personal example of such a holiday.

One Step Beyond — Create An Activity
Exercise E

Choose a paragraph from a newspaper, magazine, or novel. Copy the paragraph onto a page, replacing each verb in the text with the simple infinitive (verb without "to") in parentheses. Exchange your activity with a classmate and write the simple infinitive verbs in an appropriate tense.

Narrative/Descriptive Essays

Descriptive Essays
The descriptive essay, like the descriptive paragraph, describes a person, a place, an object, or an event in great detail so that the reader can clearly picture what is being described. An essay is used in preference to a paragraph when the topic is somewhat complex and would benefit from a lengthier, fuller, more detailed description.

Narrative Essays
The narrative essay, like the narrative paragraph, tells a story. The events can be real or fictional, but the story must illustrate a point the writer is making. The paragraphs should be arranged logically in a chronological order.

Exercise A

Reread "The Town Mouse and The Country Mouse" on page 88 and divide the story into eight main events. List the events in the order that they happen.

1. _____
2. _____
3. _____
4. _____
5. _____
6. _____
7. _____
8. _____

Exercise B

Find a colour photo in a magazine (perhaps a vacation spot in a travel magazine) of a place that you find interesting. Look at the photo and imagine that you are there. Under each "sense" listed below, write precise descriptive words or phrases to describe what you experience when you are there.

Your reader will get a much clearer "picture" of your description if you include detailed sensory images. Brainstorming sensory images is useful at the outline stage.

sight:_____

_____

_____

colours:_____

_____

_____

sound:_____

_____

_____

smell:_____

_____

_____

taste:_____

_____

_____

physical feelings: _____

_____

_____

emotional feelings: _____

_____

_____

Exercise C

Write about one of the following topics. Use the Essay Checklist at the end of this unit to edit your work.

1. Using the six pictures in the illustration below as a guide, write a narrative essay (fable) about a merchant, his son, and a donkey. Remember to include a main point in your introduction.

2. Write a narrative essay about a special childhood memory and explain why the event was special.

3. Interview an older relative and write a narrative essay about that person's life.

4. Write a descriptive essay about someone who is much younger than you, or someone much older. Describe the person's appearance, character, and behaviours.

5. Write a descriptive essay. Describe, in detail, one of the following places:

   a) a crowded shopping mall

   b) your grandparents' house or apartment

   c) an airport terminal

   d) a children's playground

☑ Essay Checklist

Outline Checklist

☐ Did I brainstorm ideas?

☐ Does my essay have a title?

☐ Have I identified my audience?

☐ Is my topic sufficiently narrowed?

☐ Have I eliminated ideas that don't relate?

☐ Does my thesis statement contain a controlling idea (attitude)?

☐ Do the topic sentences in the body support my thesis?

☐ Do I have at least 2-3 points to illustrate the main point made in each of my topic sentences?

Introductory Paragraph Checklist

☐ Will the paragraph get the reader's attention?

☐ Does the paragraph contain a thesis statement?

☐ Does the paragraph use one of these four main approaches: attention-grabber, quotation, opposite, cone?

☐ Does the introductory paragraph provide some background information?

☐ Does the introductory paragraph indicate the kind of essay that will be developed?

☐ Does the introductory paragraph indicate my point of view?

Body Paragraphs Checklist

☐ Does my paragraph have a topic sentence that supports one aspect of the thesis statement?

☐ Have I given information that supports my topic sentence?

☐ Is my paragraph unified?

☐ Does my paragraph contain a transitional sentence?

Conclusion Paragraph Checklist

☐ Does my paragraph restate, summarize, or refer to the thesis statement?

☐ Have I avoided introducing any new ideas in my paragraph?

☐ Have I left my reader with something to think about?

Editing Functions

☐ Are the sentences and ideas arranged logically?

☐ Have I used transitional expressions adequately and appropriately?

☐ Have I checked my essay to make sure the meaning of each sentence is clear?

☐ Have I checked my essay to make sure that I have used precise words and the correct form of words?

☐ Have I proofread my essay for errors in grammar, punctuation, and spelling?

ANSWER KEY

UNIT 1

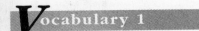

Exercise A

1. The snow was blinding, so we pulled off the road.
2. At 10:45 p.m. last night, the volcano erupted.
3. A twister touched down and destroyed everything in its path.
4. The earthquake caused great fissures.
5. The volcano emitted poisonous gases.
6. The epicentre of the earthquake was the coast of Los Angeles.
7. The aftershocks were strong enough to rattle the dishes.
8. The eye of the hurricane is calm and quiet.

Exercise B

1. drought
2. unprecedented
3. exacerbation
4. perennial
5. recurrence
6. havoc*
7. propagate
8. menacing
9. adverse
10. scourge

*Note: The verb "wreak" is commonly used with havoc.

Exercise C

strong
light   } breeze
pleasant

freezing
driving
pouring
spitting
drizzling   } rain
pelting
light
heavy

blinding
freezing
driving
pelting
powdery   } snow
light
granular
packing
heavy

strong
gale-force
light   } wind
north-easterly

Exercise D

1. mist, spitting, drizzle, downpour
2. light, powdery, packing, heavy, blinding
3. light, high, strong, gale-force

Exercise A

1. Predictions of impending doom have been issued for the past few years by scientists who study the earth's atmosphere.
2. Global warming has been caused by a gradual rise in world-wide temperatures.
3. Statements were made by individual researchers that human activity has contributed to global warming.
4. Drastic steps must be taken by the world to reduce the emissions of heat-trapping gases.
5. Huge tracts of densely-populated land will be flooded by rising oceans.
6. The effects of carbon dioxide emissions, methane, and chlorofluoro-carbons are simulated by complex computers.

Exercise B

1. Aerosols which cool the planet by blocking the sun can mask the effects of global warming.
2. Water from melting glaciers will submerge many beaches.
3. Global warming will affect temperature and rainfall patterns.
4. Deep ocean currents influence our world climate.
5. We must reduce emissions to the same levels as in the 1920s.
6. Industrialized nations must take the lead role in reducing global warming.

Exercise C

(1) location
(2) conditions
(3) characteristics
(4) processes
(5) conditions
(6) location

Exercise D

1. agent: scientists; delete
2. agent: David Suzuki; not possible to delete
3. agent: people; delete
4. agent: scientists; delete
5. agent: humans; delete

Exercise E

Possible answers:
1. Public building
2. Hospital or any public building
3. Farm or other large, privately-owned property
4. Mall or other public washroom
5. Insurance contract

Vocabulary 2 Expansion

Exercise A

1. c
2. e
3. b
4. d
5. a

Exercise B

Possible answers:
1. It's raining very hard.
2. She left him penniless.
3. Lucas misled his mother.
4. She likes to sit around and chat with her co-workers.
5. Our dream died.
6. I want to go to bed early tonight.
7. Habib risked everything to start his new business.
8. I'll accept that invitation at a future time.

Grammar Focus 2

Exercise A

Tenses (sentences will vary):
1. simple past — was / were recorded
2. simple present — am / is/ are controlled
3. present continuous — am / is being destroyed
4. past continuous — was / were being ignored
5. present perfect — has been observed
6. past perfect — had been decided
7. future — will be developed

Exercise B

1. A myth about five beautiful maidens was created by the First Nations peoples to explain the origin of Niagara Falls.
2. Anishiniba was given back his life by a wild boar.
3. Ayers Rock is considered a spiritual place by the Aboriginal people of Australia.
4. Blocks were carved out of snow by the Inuit to build igloos.
5. The weather is controlled by powerful spirits.

Exercise C

(1) is
(2) be taught
(3) become
(4) makes
(5) be
(6) be developed and studied
(7) unlearn
(8) be taken
(9) be embraced

Exercise D

1. Separate all papers.
2. Put all bottles, cans, and jars in the recycling box.
3. Use reusable cotton bags for groceries.
4. Place food scraps in a composter.
5. Use cloth diapers.
6. Donate unwanted items to charities.

Grammar Expansion

Exercise E

1. gets / is
2. gets / is
3. got / was
4. was
5. got / was

Exercises F and G — Answers will vary.

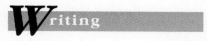
Writing

Exercise A

1. The economic damage is still being calculated
2. Farmers lost a lifetime of work
3. The army played a key role
4. Volunteers helped in any way they could

Exercise B

2, 5

Exercise C

1. first sentence
2. last sentence

Exercise D — Answers will vary.

UNIT 2

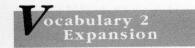

Vocabulary 1

Exercise A

(1) psychic
(2) astrology
(3) numerology
(4) clairvoyance
(5) telepathy
(6) subconscious
(7) reincarnation

Exercise B

Clues Across

1. levitate
2. omens
3. curse
4. voodoo
5. apparitions
6. psychokinetic
7. medium
8. seance

Clues Down

1. poltergeist
2. telepathy
3. shaman
4. premonitions

Exercise C — Answers will vary.

Vocabulary 2 Expansion

Exercise A

1. posthypnotic: after hypnosis
   posthumously: after death
   post- = after, behind, following
2. demystify: take away the mystery
   demean: put down
   de- = down, from, away, off
3. transcend: go beyond
   transmit: send across
   trans- = across, beyond
4. monotheistic: believing in one god
   monotonous: dull and never changing (from monotone: a single sound that never varies)
   mono- = one, alone
5. dissatisfied: not satisfied
   discredited: not respected anymore
   dis- = apart from, separate, loss of, not
6. malediction: curse (words meant to bring harm)
   malicious — bad, harmful
   mal- = bad, wrong

Exercise B — Answers will vary.

Exercise C

Possible answers (arranged alphabetically by prefix):
decaffeinated, decode, deformed, deport
disarrange, disreputable, disfigure, dishonest, disagree
malformed, maladjusted
monogram
parapsychology, paraphrase
postsecondary, postscript
prearrange, premature, preview, prefigure
subheading, subhuman
superhuman, supernova, superscript
rearrange, review, reformed, readjusted, report, replant, rephrase
telegram, telemarketing
transmission, transcript, transport, transplant

Grammar Focus 1

Exercise A

Note: Answers may vary according to the interpretation of the context in which these statements were made.

1. Ms. H. admitted that a few ghosts from her past had come back to haunt her.
   Ms. H. admitted that a few ghosts from her past have come back to haunt her.
2. Mr. B. said that there had been many unexplained events in that government last year.
3. Mr. J. was overheard saying that he believed the leader had been a fox in his previous life.
4. Mr. M. predicted that his party would balance the budget this year.
5. Mr. P. assured voters that he was learning to speak a second language because he had discovered that being unilingual in a bilingual country was a curse.
6. Mr. J. announced that he envisions a country his children and grandchildren could be proud of.
   Mr. J. announced that he envisioned a country his children and grandchildren could be proud of.
7. Mr. L. said that one didn't have to be a psychic to know that governing a bilingual country would continue to be a challenge in the future.
   Mr. L. said that one doesn't have to be a psychic to know that governing a bilingual country will continue to be a challenge in the future.

Exercise B

Possible answers:

Jerome Harrold:	"Dr. Marilyn Boch reported seeing a spaceship-like object at about 10:15 p.m. on Tuesday night."
Jerome Harrold:	"I am sceptical about the sighting despite the photographs."
Jerome Harrold:	"Perhaps Dr. Boch has been watching too many episodes of *The X- Files*."
Jerome Harrold:	"The Academy will hold a complete investigation into the sighting."
Dr. Marilyn Boch:	"I was working in the Academy's observatory when I saw a gold, oval-shaped flying machine racing through the night sky."
Dr. Marilyn Boch:	"Sightings of this nature are quite common but rarely reported."

Dr. Marilyn Boch: "Other scientists have also seen UFOs but have not reported them because they don't want to jeopardize their reputations."

Dr. Marilyn Boch: "The government is putting pressure on the scientific community to withhold information about UFO sightings in order to avoid mass panic."

Grammar Focus 2

Exercise A

The interviewer asked Noel...

1. ...how often he read his horoscope.
2. ...if he had ever had paranormal experiences.
3. ...how many supernatural phenomena he had experienced in his life.
4. ...if he knew what "psychokinesis" was.
5. ...when he had experienced his most recent paranormal experience.
6. ...if he thought he was psychic. / ...if he thinks he is psychic.
7. ...if he would participate in / consider participating in an experiment involving levitation.
8. ...if he would call the office to confirm the time of the experiment.

Exercise B

Possible answers:

1. The boy on the terrace shouted that Daniel was just in time to play ball.
2. Daniel's friends asked him if he was alright.
3. José's mother told him that the people who lived in the house were on vacation and that they had left their keys with José's parents.
4. José's father said that Daniel must have landed on the old chair and that the old chair had broken his fall.
5. At first, Daniel thought it had been a great coincidence. Later, he concluded that his guardian angel had moved that chair from somewhere else to save his life.

Exercise C — Answers will vary.

Grammar Expansion

Exercise D

1. The father shouted to his son to stop the nonsense.
2. "Do not be afraid," the shaman told him.
3. "Be careful!" said the clairvoyant.
4. She ordered her husband to get the camera.
5. The medium warned the listeners to beware of a man with a blond beard.

Exercise E — Answers will vary.

Writing

Exercise A

7, 4, 6, 8, 2, 5, 10, 3, 1, 9 or
7, 5, 4, 8, 2, 3, 10, 6, 1, 9

Exercises B and C — Answers will vary.

Editing

Exercise D

What I remember most about my arrival in this country was a feeling of hope. We arrived early one ice-cold winter morning in February. My mother and father were very exhausted, having travelled for so long with four young children. I was ten. When we stepped off the plane and looked around us at the grey, icy terminal buildings, my father said that he <u>was</u> not sure he <u>would be able to / could</u> live here. My mother took his hand and <u>told</u> him not to judge a whole country on its international airport. Still, my father insisted he <u>could</u> feel heaviness in <u>his</u> bones. "We <u>will</u> struggle here," he said. We children were very excited despite our lack of sleep and sadness at having left behind friends and relations. But on the walk from the plane to the terminal I felt a deep, cold chill creeping through my thin sweater. I began to feel tired, very tired and at that moment I cursed under my breath that perhaps my father <u>was</u> right. Perhaps we had made a mistake. My mother must have guessed my thoughts for she hugged me warmly, and looking into my innocent eyes, soothed me, saying that our arrival <u>was / had been</u> a blessing. With tears in my eyes, I looked up at <u>her</u> face. As I glanced beyond her shoulders, a faint but steady ray of sunshine was creeping through a crack in the thick winter clouds. It felt warm and soothing. I recognized it as an omen, and, as the weak sun bathed my face, I knew that she was right. Our arrival <u>was</u> a blessing. Taking my father's hand, I walked towards the terminal building with a sense of renewed hope.

Exercise E — Answers will vary.

UNIT 3

Exercise A

CATEGORY	DETERMINER	SIZE	GENERAL DESCRIPTION	AGE	SHAPE	COLOUR	MATERIAL	ORIGIN	PURPOSE
EXAMPLE	many	medium-sized		ancient			stone		
1	single	small	intricately-carved			black	onyx		fertility
2	three	colossal	majestic		pointy	blue-hazed			
3	hundreds	small	pristine			crystal-clear			
4	countless		interesting			rust-coloured		Aboriginal	religious
5	their	large	formerly-grand	ancient	dome-shaped				

Exercise B

(1) adventurous nature
(2) moderately-long, scenic
(3) Narrow, curving, man-made
(4) small, natural
(5) heavy, waterproof
(6) countless, unusual
(7) vast, white, sandy
(8) large, ten-year-old wood

Exercise C

Possible answers:
1. a distinctive, hand-carved, wooden, West Coast Native mask
2. a large, painted, cone-shaped teepee
3. a long, sturdy, Inuit kayak
4. a small, thin, dressed Native doll
5. an intricately-embroidered, dark-coloured Native dress

Exercise D

1. razor
2. dog food
3. ice cream / milkshake / frozen yogurt
4. dishwashing liquid
5. liquid refreshment (pop, etc.)

6. clothing
7. cookware
8. soap
9. paint
10. doll

Exercises E and F — Answers will vary.

Vocabulary 1

Exercise A

stimulate ⟹ inspire
who refuse to give up ⟹ persevere
without fear ⟹ bravely
willing to take risks in order to experience new situations ⟹ adventurous
devoted ⟹ dedicated
bravery ⟹ courage

Exercise B

Noun	Verb	Adjective	Adverb
bravery	brave	brave	bravely
adventure		adventurous	adventurously
dedication	dedicate	dedicated	
courage		courageous	courageously
inspiration	inspire	inspirational/ inspired/ inspiring	
perseverance	persevere	persevering	

Exercise C

Possible answers:
1. densely populated, well-maintained
2. spectacular piece of expressive architecture
3. delicately spiced
4. hospitable
5. minuscule, yet intricately carved
6. lively, entertaining, and very skillful
7. distinguished-looking
8. smooth and uneventful
9. frigid
10. awe-inspiring

Vocabulary Expansion

Exercise D

Possible answers:
1. Switzerland is considerably more expensive than Mexico.
2. Thai food is a bit hotter than Indonesian food.
3. The Japanese bullet train is substantially faster than the express train.
4. First class is much more comfortable than economy airline seats.
5. The temperature in Ecuador is slightly warmer than the temperature in southern Colombia.

Grammar Focus 2

Exercise A

1. that / which
2. which
3. whom / that
4. which
5. which
6. which
7. who / that

Exercise B

Possible answers:
1. Barb, who had never been out of Canada, flew to Thailand.
2. There, she met her sister, who had been living in Japan.
3. They enjoyed the food, which was hot and spicy.
4. They slept in guest houses that were clean, cheap, and comfortable.
5. In the market, she bought a beautiful tapestry at a good price, over which she had haggled.
6. Barb rode an elephant, which could carry two people, while trekking in northern Thailand.
7. The sisters, who had a lot of catching up to do, had a great time.
8. They saw some traditional dancers, who were very skilled and graceful.
9. The temples, which were extremely ornate, were awe-inspiring.
10. It was a great experience which she will probably never have the opportunity to repeat.

Exercise C

Possible answers:
1. ...enjoys travelling to faraway parts of the world.
2. ...have unusual architecture and museums with exhibits of cultural interest.
3. ...look unusual but appetizing.
4. ...don't have enough food to eat.
5. ...I haven't visited is India.
6. ...capture the lives of everyday people.
7. ...few tourists have been before.
8. ...the temperature is consistently over 40 degrees.

Grammar Expansion

Exercise D

The following words should be crossed out:
1. that (direct object)
2. whom (object of preposition)
3. not possible
4. who is (relative clause contains relative pronoun + *be*)
5. that (indirect object)
6. that (direct object)
7. not possible
8. which (direct object)

Exercise E

(7-9) England, where the manicured countryside was the opposite of everything I imagined as wild, (NR)

(10-11) places where there were no roads, towns or railways (R)

(27-28) fjords that carved into Baffin's northeastern coast (R)

(28-30) jigsaw puzzle.,that straddles the island's midsection (R)

(47) day when a blizzard confined us to our tents (R)

(52-53) mother, who may be nearby, (NR)

(55-56) −41°C,.,which turns Mike's beard a frosty white, (NR)

(72-74) mosquitoes that swarm around us as soon as we leave the ice cap... (R)

(78-80) route..that has been used since the first people migrated to Baffin from Alaska some 3500 years ago (R)

Reduced Relative Clauses:

(19)   tracks crisscrossing the snow (R)

(65-66)   kayaks, delivered to us by a floatplane, (NR)

(90-91)   lesson Bob and I learn in late September (R)

(95)   huffs — signal of a possible attack (NR)

(102)   tip of the island, our final goal. (NR)

(106-107) cliffs painted rust red with lichens (R)

(108-109) rafts..shoved by storm waves against the rocky shore of Nettling Lake (R)

Exercise F

Possible answers:

1. The polar bear that was trying to protect her cub huffed at the men.
2. The expedition, which lasted 192 days, was John Dunn's experience of a lifetime.
3. The temperature, which reached minus 42° F [–41°C], made it difficult to keep warm.
4. The kayaks, which were portable, were delivered by a floatplane.
5. The first people who migrated to Baffin came from Alaska.
6. They reached the southern tip of Baffin, which was their goal, in 192 days.
7. Their memories, which will last a lifetime, are a small reward for their efforts.
8. Bob Saunders, who accompanied John Dunn, completed the entire journey.

Exercise A

1. be in danger of losing everything
2. try very hard; try one's best
3. have no specific plan in mind; do things as they come
4. about to quit; totally exhausted
5. to fail
6. what interests some may not interest others

Exercise B

1. play it by ear
2. different strokes for different folks
3. gave it his best shot
4. on its last legs
5. on the line
6. blow it

Exercise A

The following sentences should be eliminated:
- Australia is a former British penal colony.
- Sydney is located in the state of New South Wales.
- Opera music can be truly inspirational, although some say it is an acquired taste.

Exercise B

Topic Sentence: As you look down Main Street towards the hotel in Banff, Alberta, you can't help but admire the beauty of this small quaint town nestled at the base of scenic mountains.

Exercise C — Answers will vary.

Exercises D and E — Answers will vary.

UNIT 4

Vocabulary 1

Exercise A

a) to understand, to comprehend, to catch something, to catch someone's drift
b) to not understand, to not get the main idea
c) to get off topic, to get off track, to talk about something unrelated, to move away from the original topic
d) to avoid saying something directly, to not get to the point
e) to discover through gossip, to hear a rumour
f) to force a comment, to make someone tell something, to get someone to be precise

Vocabulary Expansion

Exercise B

broach the subject — begin to talk about the subject
rattled on about — talked incessantly
catch my drift — understand my meaning
mark my words — listen carefully to what I'm saying and remember for future reference
mum's the word — keep quiet about something

Grammar Focus 1

Exercise A

Possible answers:
1. even though / although
2. but / yet
3. despite
4. in spite of the fact that / although / even though
5. whereas / while
6. whereas / while
7. although / even though / yet

Exercise B — Answers will vary.

Vocabulary 2

Exercise A

Incorrect	Correct
1. challenging	concise
2. photocopying	interpersonal
3. supervisor	barrier
4. computers	cues
5. lazy	vague
6. paper clips	feedback
7. wrote	gestured
8. inappropriate	perceptive
9. unfortunate	interactive
10. briefcase	message

Grammar Focus 2

Exercise A

Note: Sentence structure will vary depending on the expressions used.
1. even so / still / nevertheless / nonetheless
2. on the contrary
3. however / nevertheless / nonetheless
4. on the other hand / however
5. still / nonetheless / nevertheless
6. however / still / even so
7. however / still / even so / nonetheless / nevertheless

Grammar Expansion

Exercise B

1. (20) to establish a general feeling or atmosphere
2. (27) to do something without fail or with great commitment
3. (44-45) get off to a bad start
4. (45-46) to have a good relationship with someone
5. (51-52) to not be kept informed about things
6. (68) people who work with figures (accountants)
7. (75) to be available for people at all times
8. (80) to take care of someone/to guide someone's actions so closely that you are almost doing the action yourself
9. (92) to gossip about someone

Exercise C

1. but: lines 11, 17, 106
    yet: 101
2. although: 75
    while: 32, 67, 82, 97
    whereas: 12
    in spite of the fact that: 106
3. however: 70
    on the contrary: 110
    even so: 50
    on the other hand: 90
    still: 45 (Not used here with the meaning "despite that", but rather with the meaning of "continuing".)

Exercise D

Possible answers:

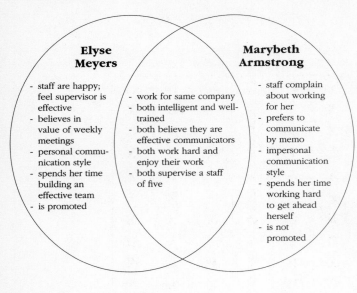

Elyse Meyers
- staff are happy; feel supervisor is effective
- believes in value of weekly meetings
- personal communication style
- spends her time building an effective team
- is promoted

(overlap)
- work for same company
- both intelligent and well-trained
- both believe they are effective communicators
- both work hard and enjoy their work
- both supervise a staff of five

Marybeth Armstrong
- staff complain about working for her
- prefers to communicate by memo
- impersonal communication style
- spends her time working hard to get ahead herself
- is not promoted

Exercise E

Note: Sentence structure will vary depending on the expressions of contrast used.
1. Incorrect: whereas; while; on the other hand; however
2. Incorrect: but; however; still; nevertheless
3. Incorrect: whereas; while; on the other hand
4. Incorrect: in spite of the fact that; even though; although; nevertheless
5. Correct
6. Correct
7. Incorrect: while; whereas; yet; on the other hand
8. Correct
9. Correct
10. Incorrect: on the other hand; while; whereas; however

Exercise F

Possible answers:
Note: Sentence structure will vary depending on the expressions of contrast used.
1. a) A bilingual child may speak English at school, **yet** switch to Polish, Spanish, or Cantonese at home.
   b) **Although** a bilingual child may speak English at school, he or she may switch to Polish, Spanish, or Cantonese at home.
   c) A bilingual child may speak English at school, **whereas** he or she may switch to Polish, Spanish, or Cantonese at home.
2. a) In one study on...learned English well **while** students who were taught different subjects....
   b) In one study on...learned English well. Students who were taught different...did not learn English well, **however**.
   c) In one study on...learned English well. **On the other hand**, students who were taught different subjects....

3. a) **Even though** it is more difficult to learn a second language in adulthood, it is not impossible.
   b) **Though** it is more difficult to learn a second language in adulthood, it is not impossible.
   c) It is more difficult to learn a second language in adulthood. **Nonetheless**, it is not impossible.
4. a) Sari Kristiina moved to North America in her forties without having learned any English. **Even so**, she managed to learn English with native-like fluency.
   b) **In spite of the fact that** Sari Kristiina moved to North America in her forties without having learned any English, she managed to learn English with native-like fluency.
   c) Sari Kristiina moved to North America in her forties without having learned any English. **Still**, she managed to learn English with native-like fluency.

Vocabulary Expansion

Exercise A

Speaking: blurt out, cut off, bite your tongue
Listening: listen up, tune in, tune out
Vocabulary: buzz-word
Understanding: grasp

Exercise B

1. bit my tongue
2. tunes out
3. cut off
4. blurted out
5. grasp
6. buzz-word
7. Listen up!
8. tuned in to

Writing

Exercise A

Point-by-point method.

Exercises B–C — Answers will vary.

UNIT 5

Vocabulary 1

Exercise A

R	B	R	C	O	N	C	E	I	V	E	D	X	N	X
X	I	X	E	X	T	X	X	X	X	X	O	X	O	X
X	N	G	C	S	X	X	X	X	X	T	X	X	N	X
E	A	Y	O	X	T	X	X	A	L	I	E	N	S	X
V	R	Y	N	R	S	O	X	X	X	N	X	S	E	L
I	Y	X	T	E	O	X	R	X	E	G	N	D	N	S
V	X	X	I	L	X	U	X	E	X	U	O	N	S	E
R	O	R	N	X	E	X	S	X	D	I	I	A	I	U
U	E	X	U	X	X	V	X	X	X	S	T	P	C	G
S	X	X	U	X	X	G	O	X	C	H	C	X	A	A
X	X	X	M	X	X	X	X	N	X	E	I	E	L	E
F	A	N	T	A	S	T	I	C	X	D	F	X	X	L
X	X	G	N	I	T	R	O	T	S	I	D	X	X	L
X	X	X	N	X	X	X	X	X	H	X	X	X	X	O
X	P	E	R	S	N	I	C	K	E	T	Y	X	X	C

The **technology** in *Star Trek* often had some scientific validity.

Exercise B

1. fantasy
2. survival
3. novel
4. distortion
5. fictional
6. collegial
7. conception
8. rigours
9. expansion
10. restoration

Exercise C — Answers will vary.

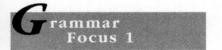

Grammar Focus 1

Exercise A

Possible answers:
1. I learned that Roddenberry attempted to make the show as realistic as possible.
2. I have learned that Roddenberry hired scientists to ensure the validity of the science portrayed.
3. I have realized that the show appeals to all types of people.
4. I learned that spaceships can't fly faster than the speed of light, and you can't hold your breath to stay conscious when in a vacuum.
5. I no longer believe the show is entirely based on fantasy.
6. I feel that the most appealing aspect of the show for Dr. Batchelor is its attempt at scientific accuracy.

Exercise B

Possible answers:
1. ...*Star Trek* initially bombed during its first three seasons...
2. ...children could watch it every day.
3. ...the show had developed a huge following.
4. ...Roddenberry's vision of the future was extremely profitable.

Exercise C

1. Lee is unaware of where the filming will take place.
2. You will be impressed by how many returning stars we have signed.
3. Do you know why she watches the show?
4. Are you aware of when the publicity campaign will kick off?
5. I can't identify who the best actor on the show is.

Exercise D

Possible answers:
1. ...I would want to watch the same show several times.
2. ...I find the shows appealing.
3. ...the attraction was.
4. ...the shows had been on the air.
5. ...the show had first started.
6. ...people would react to his pilot.
7. ...much money he would make.
8. ...the appeal of a show like *Star Trek* really is.

Grammar Expansion

Exercise E

Possible answers:

1. I'm afraid not. I don't really get into all the hype.
2. I imagine so. It takes a certain kind of personality to get totally addicted to a show.
3. I think so. I seem to remember seeing pictures on the news last year.
4. I suppose so. The captain did always have his share of beautiful women to romance.
5. I hope not. I'm tired of all the spin-offs.
6. I think so. The shows are generally not too graphically violent.

Exercise F

Noun clauses:

1) that science is tentative, that it is not certain, that it is subject to change
2) what people had not found before / what I was told to learn
3) that technological advances would benefit mankind

Vocabulary 1

Exercise A

(1) debate about
(3) degrees in
(10) samples of
(11) analysis of
(13) examination of
(16) articles about

Exercise B — Answers will vary.

Vocabulary Expansion

Exercise C

Idioms	Meaning
be under pressure	suffering from stress
burn the midnight oil	stay up very late to work
roll up one's sleeves and dig in	work hard
figure out	understand, determine
find out	discover
out of the blue	unexpectedly
in the nick of time	at the last moment

Grammar Focus 2

Exercise A

1. ...that governments have strict regulations about how far scientists can go (*it* + *be* + a + noun + noun clause)
2. That aliens have visited earth... (subject)
3. ...that we could limit human cloning to replacement parts for people... (after a noun)
4. ...that we will be making regular trips to Mars in the near future. (complement of *be*)
5. ...that scientists will try to clone humans in the future. (*it* + *seems* + adjective + noun clause)
6. ...who was responsible for the mix-up. (after a preposition)
7. ...that his view of the future would be shared by others. (after an adjective of feeling or opinion)

Exercise B

Possible answers:

1. That computers are taking over some people's jobs worries me.
2. Whether humans are cloned or not is of concern to everyone.
3. That people have reported sightings of UFOs supports the notion that there is life on other planets.
4. That people reacted so strongly to Dolly demonstrates that many people are uncomfortable with gene manipulation.
5. That jobs are being lost due to technological change is a huge problem.
6. That there is life on other planets is not universally accepted.

Exercise C

Possible answers:

1. The fact that police must now monitor the Internet is pathetic.
2. The idea that a computer could be portable was inconceivable 35 years ago.
3. The discovery that hydrogen and oxygen can be combined to make a clean fuel for our future is fantastic.
4. The news that malfunctioning genes may be repaired in the future has given hope to many individuals.
5. The idea that you can take an exotic vacation without leaving home appeals to some people.

Exercise D

Possible answers:

1. I am especially interested in what the mission to Mars will reveal about the possibilities of life on that planet.
2. Do you honestly approve of what scientists are doing with genetic manipulation?
3. The studies focus on whether or not life is possible on Mars.
4. In the future they will look at the possibility that cities could be built on Mars.
5. People cannot rely on what they hear or read in media reports about UFOs.
6. Do you agree with who they want to send on the first mission to Mars?

Exercise E

1. People asked why the scientists wanted to do this type of experiment.
2. The scientists indicated to them that they hoped to gain insights into cell growth.
3. The people asked the scientists if they had considered the possible negative implications.
4. According to the scientists, it was important that this type of research be done despite the possible negative implications.
5. The people told the scientists that they would like to see genetic manipulation stopped immediately.
6. What that would do is prevent scientists from creating human clones.
7. Working together, the people and scientists discussed how they could continue research in a limited way.

Vocabulary 2

Exercise A

Possible answers:

autonomy	automobile	autocracy	autocrat
autograph	automat	automation	
dynamo	dynamism	dynasty	dynamic
astronomy	astrological	astrologist	astrology
astrophysics	astrochemistry	astrograph	astronaut
astrophysics			
lithograph	paragraph	telegraph	photograph
biopsy	biological	biodegradable	biologist
biology	biophysics	biochemistry	biorhythm
cyclone	cyclometer		
pathological	pathologist	pathology	pathogen
geological	geologist	geology	geocentric
geometry	geophysics	geopolitics	

Exercise B — Answers will vary.

Writing

Exercise A

Possible answers:

Outline 1. Automation has resulted in the need for fewer workers.

Outline 2. Many celebrities do what they can to help in the fight against AIDS.

Exercise B

Controlling ideas:

1. ...enabled us to explore areas where no human has visited
2. ...gone too far
3. ...successful spin-offs

Exercise C

1. Cloning has been a popular subject for Hollywood movies.
2. popular subject for Hollywood movies.
3. Examples are sequenced from past to most recent.
4. a. Initially, scientists attempted to create their own being by replicating body parts in *Frankenstein* movies.
   b. Then, a number of blue-eyed, black-haired boys from the skin and blood of Adolf Hitler were created in *The Boys From Brazil*.
   c. Finally, there is the construction foreman who replicates himself with the help of a local geneticist in *Multiplicity*.

Editing

Exercise D

Outline 1

Topic Sentence: Downsizing in companies as a result of technological advances has had a tremendous personal impact on workers.

Example 1: It is a fact that many men in their late fifties who have been laid off have been unable to rejoin the workforce, and consequently lose everything they ever had.

Example 2: It's the idea that they are no longer useful that leads some men into personal depression.

Example 3: It's been documented that men who lose their jobs sometimes have serious problems with their families.

Outline 2

Topic Sentence: Advances in technology have created increasingly destructive weapons of war.

Example 1: That soldiers could only kill when at arm's length from each other had limited casualties to some extent.

Example 2: The fact that guns enabled soldiers to kill at great distances increased the bloodshed in conflicts incredibly.

Example 3: The fact that nuclear bombs can instantly annihilate everything within a wide radius of landing has brought unlimited killing capacity to war.

Exercises E and F — Answers will vary.

UNIT 6

Vocabulary 1

Exercise A

(2)   reason
(4)   conclusions
(5)   analogies
(15)   deduction
(39)   ingenuity
(39)   rational
(41)   Ignorance

Exercise B

1. physical
2. knowledgeable
3. opinion
4. wisdom
5. riddle
6. spatial
7. argument
8. puzzled

Grammar Focus 1

Exercise A

1. g
2. e
3. d
4. a
5. h
6. b
7. f
8. c

Exercise B

1. (I) ... if my parents had encouraged me more/I would do better in school
2. (C)
3. (I) ... his intellect would develop more/If the parents had provided a more stimulating environment
4. (I) ... if they read a variety of materials
5. (C)
6. (I) ... half the battle is won
7. (C)

Exercise C

1. If Randa didn't value education, she wouldn't study so hard.
2. If Peter had not been interested in science as a young man, he wouldn't (might not) have become an engineer.
3. If Margaret weren't a teacher, she wouldn't know what will be expected of her children when they get to high school.
4. If Cosmo had liked to write, he would have written more often.
5. If Tina didn't take her young daughter Chloë to the library every week, Chloë wouldn't feel so comfortable there.

6. If Chris hadn't begun piano lessons at the age of four, now, at the age of six, he wouldn't play so well.
7. If Nicholas weren't so interested in science, his mother would not have sent him to science camp in the summer.
8. If young Martin didn't spend so much time with his Spanish-speaking grandparents, he wouldn't speak Spanish as well as English.

Exercise D — Answers will vary.

Vocabulary 2

Exercise A

(1) focus on
(2) figure out
(3) find out
(4) working towards
(5) accounted for
(6) bring about

Exercise B

1.	*to focus:*	to adjust a lens in order to see clearly; to make clear
		to direct something onto a point
	to focus on:	to concentrate on
		to direct attention to
2.	*to figure:*	to believe, think, conclude
	to figure out:	to discover
		to think about until you understand
3.	*to account:*	to think or consider (e.g., She accounted him a good writer.)
	to account for:	to explain
4.	*to work:*	to have a job
		to make an effort to do something
		to function, operate, control
	to work towards:	to try to reach or achieve a goal
5.	*to bring:*	to cause to come
		to carry to
	to bring about:	to make something happen
6.	*to find:*	to look for and get back after a search
		to get or discover after a search
	to find out:	to learn by study or inquiry
		to discover

Exercise C — Answers will vary.

Grammar Focus 2

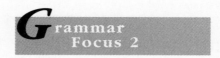

Exercise A

a. The victim must have screamed.
b. The cook could have killed him.
c. The maid might have seen the murderer.
d. The wife probably didn't kill him.
e. The president couldn't have committed suicide./The president didn't commit suicide.

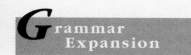

Grammar Expansion

Exercise B

Possible answers:

1. If you want to do well on the test, you will have to study hard.
2. If you know one foreign language, it should be easier to learn another.
3. If you don't read the book, you will not be able to write the summary.
4. If the suspect has an alibi, he can't have committed the murder. / If the suspect can't supply an alibi, he might have committed the murder.
5. If you knew something about the American Civil Rights Movement, you might understand the context of Martin Luther King's speech better.

Exercise C

1. If you are trying to solve a problem, your first step should be to interpret or represent the problem correctly.
2. The "tactic of elimination" strategy will only work if your list of possible solutions contains at least one good solution to the problem.
3. If the "tactic of elimination" strategy is not suitable for solving a problem, you can try visualizing or creative problem-solving.
4. If you cannot find a solution to a problem after careful, step-by-step efforts, you should stop thinking about the problem for a while and return to it later, approaching it from a new angle.
5. If you reject a prospective solution at first glance, you may be rejecting a solution that may solve your problem.

Exercise D

Note: Some variations may exist according to interpretation of context.

1. If all carnivores eat meat, and my pet is a carnivore, then my pet must eat meat.
2. If polar bears are white, and this bear lives at the North Pole, then this bear must be white.
3. If Henry lost his dog that answers to the name of Fado, and Jeannie found a dog that answers to the name of Fado, then the dog Jeannie found might be the dog Henry lost.
4. If Martin's grandparents speak only Spanish, and Martin spends a lot of time with them, then he probably speaks (might speak) Spanish too.
5. If you have no brothers or sisters, and this man is your father's son, then this man must be you.
6. If the mystery word has three letters, is a synonym for "happy," and does not contain the letter "j", then the mystery word cannot be "joy."
7. If the teacher received an essay from an unidentified student about the American Civil Rights Movement, only two students wrote an essay on this topic, and John wrote an essay on the great explosion at Halifax Harbour in 1917, then John did not write the essay on the American Civil Rights Movement.
8. If Anita's mother is Francophone, Anita lives in Edmonton where English is spoken, but Anita speaks English and French, she might have learned French from her mother.

Exercise E — Answers will vary.

Vocabulary Expansion

Exercise A

Cause: (5, 23) source of, (18) imposed (by), (14, 19) result from, (25, 27) because (of)
Effect: (11) lead to, (14) result in, (15) forced to

Additional expressions
Cause: caused by, reasons for
Effect: consequence of

Exercise B — Answers will vary.

Writing

Exercises A and B — Answers will vary.

Exercise C

If I teach my children only one skill, it will be to learn how to learn. In our fast-changing technological society, if one can't learn new skills quickly and adapt to new ideas, one is lost. Gone are the days when rote learning led the way to knowledge and success. As little as 50 years ago, if you were knowledgeable, you were admired. If you had a college or university degree, you were guaranteed a good job. If knowledge is all you can offer an employer today, you're not worth hiring; today's knowledge is obsolete tomorrow. However, if you know where and how to access knowledge, you have a transferable skill that will never be obsolete. If you can understand how you, as an individual, learn best and can acquire the skills for learning, your road will be paved with opportunity. If, on the other hand, you focus only on what you are learning, without ever understanding the process, each new learning experience may/will lead to frustration and possibly failure.

Exercise D — Answers will vary.

UNIT 7

Vocabulary 1

Exercise A

r	t	i	v	f	k	a	p	k	l	m
t	r	r	d	e	m	l	o	d	i	l
g	i	m	m	i	c	k	s	e	b	h
n	v	o	a	i	t	o	c	p	t	c
h	i	p	n	i	n	r	i	y	c	g
m	a	n	i	a	e	a	k	h	d	i
e	l	a	c	n	r	o	m	l	a	m
r	n	o	e	r	t	r	e	n	d	s

1. gimmicks
2. hyped
3. trivia
4. idol
5. mania
6. trends

Exercise B

idolize
trivial
crazy/crazed
gimmicky
trendy
manic
to hype

Exercise C — Answers will vary.

Grammar Focus

Exercise A

Possible answers:
1. The object of the game is to guess mystery phrases in as short a time as possible.
2. The team captains leave the room to choose up sides.
3. Teammates should try to guess the mystery phrase.
4. Players can't use their voices/props to get an idea across.
5. Players might point to people in the room to put over an idea.
6. In this game, players use gestures to act out a mystery phrase.

Exercise B

Possible answers:
1. The object of the game is to write in each space a word fitting the category and beginning with the letter of the key word at the head of that column.
2. It is difficult to find new categories.

3. The five-letter key word is chosen to indicate to players what letters they must use to begin the words in each category.
4. In this game, a time limit is set to control the length of the game and to ensure all players have equal time to write their answers.

Exercise C

Possible answers:
1. A parlour is/was a room used to entertain guests.
2. People play parlour games to relax.
3. In Charades players try to guess mystery phrases.
4. Playing word games is a good way to develop language skills.
5. It is difficult to play timed games.
6. To score high in timed games, you must be quick.

Exercise D — Answers will vary.

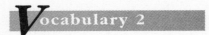
Vocabulary 2

Exercise A — Answers will vary.

Exercise B

1. obnoxious
2. outlet
3. trauma
4. folly
5. condemned
6. dysfunctional
7. omnipresent
8. opportunistic
9. pretentious
10. cope

Exercise C — Answers will vary.

Grammar Expansion

Exercise A

1. She appears not to have known the words to the song very well.
2. The stage actor seems to have forgotten his line.
3. The star was disappointed not to have won an Academy Award.
4. They were sorry to have missed the first act.
5. The people in the audience were thrilled to have persuaded the entertainer to come out on stage for an encore.
6. I'm glad to have seen Céline Dion in concert last summer.
7. It would have been fun to have been studying at a North American university during the goldfish-swallowing craze.
8. Wally and Brenda were sorry to have missed the last episode of *The X-Files*.

Exercise B

(1) to see
(2) to learn
(3) to be
(4) to get

(5) to leave for
(6) to avoid
(7) to hear
(8) to have waited
(9) to have had
(10) to have spent

Exercise C

Possible answers:
1. ...to have got lost in the mail.
2. ...to collect enough money for a nice birthday gift./ to bring pop because she left the case in the supermarket parking lot.
3. ...to deliver the cake, but the cake's icing melted in the trunk of her car.
4. ...to have been stolen from her car. (perfect passive)
5. ...to plan a birthday party for Manuela./ to book the community centre hall, but it was too expensive.
6. ...to have made such a mess of things.
7. ...Elizabeth to throw her a surprise party.
8. ...everything to go well when she made her "To Do" list./ to collect enough money from friends for a gift, but she only raised $10.

Writing

Exercise A

TITLE: The Queen of Hearts

INTRODUCTION

Thesis Statement: Born into a world of privilege, Diana naturally radiated the grace and glamour of the world's elite, yet she displayed the human qualities of the common citizen — and therein lay her immeasurable appeal.

BODY

Developmental Paragraph 1

Topic Sentence: Unlike other public figures, Diana acknowledged her faults and this gave her a genuine human quality.

Support: money spent on clothes
media manipulation
affair

Developmental Paragraph 2

Topic Sentence: Like us, Diana was burdened with hardships during her short life, a human quality that gave her distinct appeal.

Support: confined by protocol
stalked by media
hounded by public
child of broken marriage
disdain of mother-in-law
rejection by husband

Developmental Paragraph 3

Topic Sentence: The outpouring of grief — sincere grief — mirrored Diana's most desirable human qualities: she was sincere and compassionate.
Support: visit to AIDS hospice
knelt to eye level of children
raised boys with hugs and kisses

CONCLUSION

Topic Sentence: When future generations read about Princess Diana in their history books, they will read about the unique ability she had to marry the world of the nobility and the common citizen.

Concluding Idea: Through her, the public perceived the nobility as a little more human and themselves as a little more noble.

Exercises B–E — Answers will vary.

UNIT 8

Vocabulary 1

Exercise A

1. i
2. d
3. h
4. e
5. a
6. j
7. f
8. b
9. g
10. c

Exercise B

(a) bounce a few ideas (off)
(b) to tackle
(c) playing hardball
(d) clear sailing
(e) going downhill
(f) ballpark figure
(g) wrestle with the hard facts
(h) Go the distance

Vocabulary Expansion

Exercise C

1. badminton racquets
2. _ball gloves
3. _lls
4.

_ton, and soccer.

G_

Exercise A

Possible answers:

1. I really regret not going to the game last night.
2. He has always avoided stating his opinion that hockey is a violent sport.
3. We discussed organizing a tournament for charity.
4. As a teenager, I disliked not being able to excel in sports.
5. Did they mention buying new equipment at the meeting?
6. Soccer players have to practise dribbling the ball up and down the field.
7. I can't imagine not participating in some kind of physical activity to keep fit.
8. Star athletes can't risk playing with an injury that may end their careers.

Exercise B

Possible answers:

1. I imagine playing soccer isn't that expensive.
2. People keep watching whether it is a real sport or not. I guess it depends on your definition of a real sport.
3. I can't help thinking that playing co-ed sports helps develop respect.
4. I understand participating in both kinds of sports is challenging.
5. I suggest trying synchronized swimming before making such a statement.

Exercise C

1. The figure skater increased his speed by sharpening his skates.
2. Bailey won the Olympic 100 m dash by running the fastest race of his life.
3. Ken accommodated the changing snow conditions by changing the wax on his skis.
4. Michael Chang ensured his racquet was in top shape by restringing it.
5. The baseball player ended the game by catching a fly ball.
6. Chandra won the tournament by bowling a perfect game.

Exercise D

1. Ken is concerned about being able to afford his son's hockey equipment.
2. I'm very excited about going to Wimbledon to watch the tennis finals.
3. He is very good at scoring goals.
4. Marnie McBean is really proud of having the most medals for rowing won by any Canadian.
5. The new jungle gym is very suitable for climbing and playing.
6. They are tired of always arguing when they play tennis.
7. The team is worried about winning the next game./ The team is worried about making the playoffs.
8. He's afraid of diving from the high board.

Exercise E

1. on going
2. of sitting/ of staying
3. to losing
4. at sticking
5. of failing

Exercise F

1. We can't have him draining the wading pool early.
2. I resent his (the referee) constantly making calls in favour of the other team.
3. Everyone appreciates her (Jolene) playing at the top of her game.
4. I don't mind them (the neighbourhood children) playing road hockey on our street.
5. They appreciate her (Shari) giving them swimming lessons.

Exercise G

(a) hoping	- insert at end of sentence
(b) darting / swimming	- post modifier
(c) diving / swimming	- subject
(d) rewarding / exciting	- adjective in the complement position
(e) returning	- object of preposition

Exercise H

Possible answers:

1. ...playing someone not as skilled as she is.
2. ...playing demanding sports like tennis.
3. ...socializing while playing a sport.
4. ...developing physical fitness and endurance.
5. ...taking part in strenuous sports.
6. ...participating in sports that don't give a physical workout.
7. ...having a close match.
8. ...playing a leisurely game.
9. ...improving their hand-eye coordination.
10. ...meeting potential clients on the course.

Exercise I — Answers will vary.

Vocabulary 2 Expansion

Exercise A

1. a
2. f
3. i
4. c
5. h
6. e
7. j
8. d
9. g
10. b

Exercise B

Possible answers:

Swimming: stroke, float, splash, kick, dive
Soccer: head, kick, pass, guard, dribble
Tennis: slam, run, smash, return, serve
Baseball: hit, run, slide, drive, bunt
Basketball: dribble, slam, dunk, pass, throw
Hockey: pass, skate, hit, high stick, check

Exercise C — Answers will vary.

Exercise D

Degree of Intensity	Intensifiers
A small degree	a bit, slightly, kind of, a little, a touch, sort of
A moderate degree	reasonably, rather, somewhat, pretty, quite
A large degree	very, really, substantially, much, awfully, considerably, extremely

Exercise E

Possible answers:

1. a bit
2. extremely
3. somewhat
4. a little
5. really
6. reasonably

Grammar Focus 2

Exercise A

1. rowing
2. going
3. to collect
4. playing
5. winning
6. to see

Exercise B

Possible answers:

1. She remembered to bring the football.
2. He forgot to pack the baseball bat.
3. He stopped to buy some water.
4. She regrets breaking her tennis racquet.
5. He remembered paying for the ball.
6. She forgot to pack his towel in his gym bag.

Exercise C

(a) Participating/Taking part
(b) to consider
(c) to stand
(d) to follow
(e) training
(f) hiring
(g) qualifying
(h) performing
(i) to take part/to participate

Possible answers:

1. Olympic athletes can't stop practising before a tournament or they will not make the top three.
2. It is very expensive to hire good coaches.
3. Taking part in the Olympics is a thrill of a lifetime.
4. It is important to practise, practise, practise.
5. The athletes follow a challenging training schedule.

Exercise D

Athletes keep <u>getting</u> better every year with the improvement of <u>training</u> facilities and equipment. <u>Existing</u> world records are broken on a regular basis. Many athletes, desperate <u>to win</u> the glory of the gold, turn to <u>performance-enhancing</u> drugs such as steroids and other forms of hopefully untraceable drugs. Regular drug <u>testing</u> of athletes is now a requirement in the highly competitive <u>world</u> of athletics. The number of these records that have been awarded to athletes who have managed <u>to slip</u> by the <u>testing</u> is unclear. However, what remains a little changed fact is the average age of <u>top-performing</u> athletes. In the early 1900s, the average age of gold medal winners was 25. Today, this average has changed only slightly to 24.6. This indicates that no matter what athletes do <u>to improve</u> their <u>training</u>, equipment or performance, age will probably be the most influential factor.

Possible answers:

1. ...to win gold.
2. Taking performance-enhancing drugs...
3. ...to win at any cost.
4. ...to test for drug usage.
5. ...being caught.

Exercise E — Answers will vary.

Writing

Exercise A

Paragraph 3

Exercise B

1. last sentence
2. attention grabber
3. Mike Tyson incident
4. Persuasive
5. such behaviour cannot be tolerated

Exercise C — Answers will vary.

UNIT 9

Vocabulary 1

Exercise A

1. impulsive
2. perished
3. atmospheric
4. unique
5. onslaught
6. interloper
7. tread
8. government
9. diversify
10. entice

Exercise B

A. Things that relate to **addiction**.
B. Things that relate to **obesity**.
C. Things that relate to **bingeing**.
D. Things that relate to **coping.**
E. Things that relate to **compulsion.**
F. Things that relate to **sustenance.**

Exercise C

(a) declares
(b) wiser
(c) Nutrition
(d) benefits
(e) prevailing
(f) counterproductive
(g) emerged
(h) dosage
(i) secretion
(j) substance

Exercise D

1. False. No food causes pimples; they are caused by genetics and stress.
2. True. Studies show that chicken soup makes your nose run which helps you get the cold germs out of your system.
3. False. Wearing garlic has no practical value except to maybe keep everyone away from you because of the smell.
4. True. Steaks are cold and flexible so they can conform to the face — the cold reduces the swelling and constricts broken blood vessels.
5. True. Ginger and soda both absorb acids in the stomach.
6. True. Your body burns the energy from food within four hours. After a long night's sleep, your body needs food to function well.
7. True. The vitamin A in carrots helps maintain eye tissue.
8. False. The colour of eggshell depends on the type of hen and has no effect on nutrition.
9. False. Two or three healthful snacks between meals benefit children who have high energy needs.
10. False. The alternatives do not contain any significant amount of vitamins or minerals.

Exercise E — Answers will vary.

Grammar Focus

Exercise A

1. well-known
2. fat-reduced
3. all-consuming
4. weight-reducing
5. well-trained
6. confusing
7. frequently mentioned
8. disappointing
9. prepackaged
10. hidden

Exercise B

1. Top athletes follow carefully-planned diets.
2. A much-photographed Kate Moss looks anorexic.
3. The frightening statistics indicate that death due to eating disorders is on the rise amongst teenagers.
4. My well-intentioned mother told me to watch my weight.
5. The televised debate on nutrition was insightful.
6. The surprising results made headlines around the world.

Exercise C

(5)   processed
(27-28) contained
(29)   saturated
(31)   Recommended
(35)   recommended
(39)   Proposed
(50)   accepted
(50)   qualified
(50-51) calorie-reduced
(53)   calorie-reduced
(56)   saturated

Exercise D

1. Concerned
2. approved / packaging
3. Established
4. simplified / informed
5. recommended
6. influenced
7. faced
8. utilized

Exercise E

1. descriptor of subject
2. pre-modifier / pre-modifier
3. pre-modifier
4. pre-modifier / pre-modifier
5. adjective in complement
6. post-modifier
7. post-modifier
8. post-modifier

Exercise F — Answers will vary.

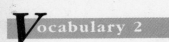

Vocabulary 2

Exercise A

Possible answers:

suffix	noun	verb	adjective	adverb
-ly	probability norm normality	like	likeable probable current virtual normal	likely (4) probably (11) currently (16)(35) especially (22) virtually (25) normally (41)
-al	nutrition option	opt	nutritional (10) optional (11)	nutritionally
-ion	information (10-11) regulations (12, 39, 52) connection (46)	inform regulate connect	informational informed/informing regulating/ regulated connecting/ connected	
-er	manufacturer (8) packager (8)	manufacture package	manufacturing/ manufactured packaging/ packaged fewer (53)	

Note: "virtually," "normally," and "optional" all contain two
    suffixes

Exercise B

Possible answers:
diet: dietician, dietary, dieter, dietetics
nature: naturally, natural, naturalize
taste: tasteless, taster, tasty, tasteful, tastefully, tastelessly
consume: consumables, consumer, consumerism, consuming,
    consumption

Exercise C — Answers will vary.

Writing

Exercises A–E — Answers will vary.

UNIT 10

Vocabulary 1

Exercise A

1. What is *resolve?*
2. What is *span?*
3. What is *apprentice?*
4. What is *strive?*
5. What is *theory?*
6. What is *evolve?*
7. What is *revolution?*
8. What is *mature?*
9. What is *develop?* (*adj.* developmental)
10. What is *turbulent?*

Exercises B–D — Answers will vary.

Grammar Focus

Exercise A

1. (I) — plays
2. (I) — took on
3. (I) — has been criticized
4. (I) — will no longer target
5. (C)
6. (I) — will likely have lived
7. (I) — deteriorate
8. (C)

Exercise B

1. develop
2. were developing/developed
3. have been developing
4. have just developed/just developed
5. is developing
6. developed
7. will be developing
8. will have developed/will be developing
9. develop/will develop
10. had been developing/was developing
11. had developed/developed
12. will have been developing

Exercise C

Note: Verb forms are listed below. Sentences will vary.
1. evolve(s)
2. will resolve
3. was/were developing
4. has/have been maturing
5. am/is/are striving
6. will be spanning
7. will have globalized
8. apprenticed
9. had theorized
10. has/have resolved
11. will have been flourishing
12. had been trying out

Vocabulary Expansion

Exercise A — Answers will vary.

Exercise B

revolve — around
evolve — into, from...to, over, for
span — over, across, from...to
strive — to, for

Grammar Expansion

Exercise A

1. Critical work in this field was done at the turn of the last century by Sigmund Freud, a trained physician, ...
2. But a study of literacy rates among different generational groups in Canada **published in 1990**, revealed...
   ...fewer people in our **parents' and grandparents' generation** had access to education.
   ...who **a few decades ago** would never have been included in mainstream education, now...
3. People want to be in control of their own lives — that's only natural.

Exercise B

(1) was
(2) can't believe
(3) flies
(4) saw
(5) had
(6) are
(7) doesn't look
(8) saw
(9) look
(10) Is
(11) looks
(12) seems
(13) announced
(14) was
(15) does the time go / has the time gone
(16) was
(17) won
(18) will be
(19) Do you believe / Can you believe
(20) married / got married
(21) was
(22) worked / were working
(23) will marry
(24) leave

Exercise C

(1) was
(2) had accepted
(3) gave
(4) had
(5) tried

(6) disliked
(7) picked
(8) tasted
(9) said
(10) stand
(11) suppose
(12) don't know
(13) don't you go
(14) have tasted/taste
(15) eat
(16) will never want
(17) forgave
(18) consented
(19) arrived
(20) took
(21) was/had been
(22) must be
(23) said
(24) Rest
(25) will bring
(26) brought
(27) thought
(28) wanted
(29) had
(30) heard
(31) saw
(32) ran
(33) found
(34) stood/was standing
(35) made
(36) could get
(37) said
(38) have
(39) are

Exercises D and E — Answers will vary.

Writing

Exercise A
Possible answers:
1. Town mouse visits his cousin in the country.
2. Country mice eat country-type food.
3. Town mouse doesn't like country-type food, and invites country mouse to the city.
4. Country mouse goes to the city.
5. Town mouse takes the country mouse to eat a fancy meal.
6. Country mouse loves the meal.
7. Things become dangerous.
8. Country mouse wants to go home.

Exercises B and C — Answers will vary.

Text Acknowledgements

pp. 10-11 (Exercise B clues): Excerpts from *Ghosts and the Supernatural* (Collins, 1989) by Pam Beasant. Reprinted by permission of the author.

pp. 14-15: 'A Cradle of Love' from *An Angel To Watch Over Me* by Joan Webster Anderson. Copyright © 1994 by Joan Webster Anderson. Reprinted by permission of Ballantine Books, a Division of Random House Inc.

pp. 24-26: Excerpts from 'Traversing Baffin Island' by John Dunn from *National Geographic*, October 1996. Reprinted by permission of John Dunn/Arctic Light.

p. 53: From Morris, Charles G., UNDERSTANDING PSYCHOLOGY, 3/e, © 1996, pp. 247-248. Reprinted by permission of Prentice Hall, Upper Saddle River, New Jersey.

pp. 76-77: Excerpt from 'Nutrition congress grapples with conflicting advice' by Karen Unland, *The Globe and Mail*, 30 July 1997. Reprinted with permission from The Globe and Mail.

p. 79: Reproduced from *Foods That Harm, Foods That Heal* copyright © 1997 The Reader's Digest Association (Canada) Ltd. Used by permission of The Reader's Digest Association (Canada) Ltd.

p. 90: Excerpt (cartoon illustration) from *Composition Through Pictures* by J.B. Heaton (Longman Group, 1996) is reprinted by permission of Addison Wesley Longman.

Information on parlour games pp. 58-59 is based on the following source:
Play According to HOYLE – Hoyles Rules of Games. Edited by Albert H. Morehead and Geoffrey Mott-Smith. New American Library, 1983, pp. 244-245

Photo Credits

p. 7 Tom Thomson/Liaison/Pono Presse

p. 19 Gloria McPherson-Ramirez

p. 20 (1) National Museums of Canada, Canadian Museum of Civilization J-9122; (2) J. Anderton/Glenbow File No. NA-408-1; (3) Royal Ontario Museum HC 2257; (4) National Museums of Canada, Canadian Museum of Civilization 74-8066; (5) National Museums of Canada, Canadian Museum of Civilization 77-6559

p. 29 Richard Hartmeir/First Light